Carousel Carving

Miniature to Full-Size

Classics & Originals

Bruce A. White

STERLING PUBLISHING CO., INC. / NEW YORK

Acknowledgments

On June 29, 2000, my workshop building burned. We lost everything, including many of our personal items that were packed for a move. Only the hard work and perseverance of Nancy Klenke and my wife Cindy salvaged my dream, which had become their dream as well. I am forever in their debt.

LIBRARY OF CONGRESS CATALOGING-IN-PUBLICATION DATA

White, Bruce A., 1956

    Carousel carving : miniature to full-size, classics & originals / Bruce A. White.

      p. cm.

    Includes bibliographical references and index.

    ISBN 0-8069-3018-7

    1. Wood-carving. 2. Merry-go-round art. 3. Animals in art. I. Title.

TT199.7 .W527 2002

731'.832—dc21   2002017740

10 9 8 7 6 5 4 3 2 1

Published by Sterling Publishing Co., Inc.

387 Park Avenue South, New York, NY 10016

© 2002 by Bruce Allen White

Distributed in Canada by Sterling Publishing

c/o Canadian Manda Group, One Atlantic Avenue, Suite 105

Toronto, Ontario, Canada M6K 3E7

Distributed in Great Britain by Chrysalis Books

64 Brewery Road, London N7 9NT, England

Distributed in Australia by Capricorn Link (Australia) Pty. Ltd.

P.O. Box 704, Windsor, NSW 2756 Australia

Printed in China

Sterling ISBN 0-8069-3018-7

Photographs by Bruce A. White,
except 1-22 and 1-23 on page 30 and 1-24 on page 31
by William Jaquith

Book design: Richard Oriolo
Editor and layout design: Rodman Pilgrim Neumann

I hold close to my heart the memory of my son as a young boy, skipping carefree and happy through the supermarket . . . in second-hand clothes and worn-out shoes. When my wife asked me what was wrong, I just mumbled some excuse.

This book is dedicated to my children: Amirina, Charity, Jacquie, Gladys, and Zachary. But most especially to my wife Cindy. Without their sacrifice and support, I would never have been able to pursue my dream as a carousel artist, which eventually resulted in the opportunity to write this book.

The Kid & the Carver

She was just two years old
when her mom lifted her onto the carousel,
She adjusted her dress, grabbed the brass pole
and the ride began to weave its spell.
She closed her eyes for a moment . . .
The moment solemn as a prayer
then her smile lit up her face
as the wind gently brushed her hair.
She giggled . . . then she laughed out loud
she was now a princess . . . this little child
riding her stallion to far away lands
where all our dreams run free and wild.
. . . That kid on the eagle
knew that he could fly
as his hands reached towards the heavens
he seemed to touch the sky.
. . . That one on the dolphin
the ocean became his home
dancing across cascading waves
wind whipping water into foam.
. . . That boy on the fierce raptor
he whooped, hollered, let out a roar
Dad, . . . Dad, . . . look at me!
I'm riding on a dinosaur!
. . . That kid on the hummingbird
fluttered through the trees
floated over wildflower meadows
and was dancing with the bees.

He looked at the wood he'd glued last week
The small chainsaw was silent by his side
that first cut still brought a thrill
. . . the beginning of a carousel ride,
He closed his eyes for a moment
and he whispered a little prayer
. . . "When they sit on this one Lord
Let their worries be left behind
Let their hearts beat again as a little child
Let them ride without a care
Let them smile for just a moment . . .
As you make their dreams run free and wild."
The chainsaw threw chips and spots of oil
the mallet and chisel echoed through the night
the days turned into weeks and weekends
fingers danced with sandpaper to get it right
. . . Let them fly, Lord
Let them soar
Let them ride the oceans
And hear the waters roar.
Take them to exotic places
Let them know as they play their part,
"You can become what you believe"
Lord, write it on their heart
The carver's tools were laid aside
He took one last look after the paint had dried
patted it gently as he walked away
. . . the beginning of a carousel ride.

He watched her smile, he caught her look in the corner of his eye
He thought, Lord, she's the reason I do this . . . as he smiles too,
A weathered hand brushes a single tear . . . and he simply says . . . thank you.

— Pete Fedder (Read twice; first by columns, then line by line across the columns.
There are two poems with slightly different meanings.)

∽ Contents ∾

✨ *Preface* ✨

In my own work I imagine I am creating dream weavers. What in the world is a dream weaver? The next time you watch children riding on a carousel, merry-go-round, carry-us-all—whatever you want to call the machine—you will know what I mean. By whatever name you wish to call it, it is a dream weaver. Just watch and listen to the children as they ride

their majestic steeds around and around, up and down, as the machine weaves its magical spell. You might just start weaving a few dreams of your own.

"Carousel" was originally a French word used to describe a flamboyant pageant and parade, the horses and other animals richly adorned, proudly prancing to the music before the lights and mirrors. "Merry-go-round" is an English term, coined perhaps as early as 1729 by the poet George Alexander Stevens describing the St. Bartholomew fair.

Another British term is "roundabout." And C. W. Parker coined the American term "carry-us-all." No matter who you are, where you are from, or what your age, his magic machine will "carry-us-all" to wherever our imaginations take us.

Whatever you want to call these magic machines and the creatures that populate them, happiness seems to be one of the defining terms. I know that my carousel makes happy not only the children and the young at heart who ride it, it makes me happy. Why don't you let me show you how the great masters of the past made their "dream weavers" and how you can make one of your own.

Carousels have been around for a long while, developed in one form or another independently in various parts of the world. The carousel as we know it developed in the late seventeenth century and flourished only to fade with the advent of other amusements in the mid-twentieth century.

The widespread interest in carousels and their history that is so palpable now in the early twenty-first century owes its renaissance to the late 1970s. It was then that interest began to be rekindled in the highly artistic machines and the animal figures they bear. This growing interest was sparked in no small measure by Frederick Fried's book, *A Pictorial History of the Carousel* (1964, Vestal Press, Ltd., Vestal, New York). But there was a negative side to this renewed interest. The old machines were often broken up and the animals auctioned off to the highest bidders. The frameworks of the machines, often works of art as priceless as the figures mounted on them, were most commonly destroyed. The individual figures often fetched tens of thousands of dollars. This, of course, puts this beautiful art form out of reach of the common man, and most often out of sight as well, as they are in private collections.

The circa 1900 German carousel for which I have been carving new figures, funded by the National Foundation for Carnival Heritage, was brought over from Germany in 1988. The 32 horses it originally bore were auctioned off for a total of more than one million dollars. The machine was going to be burned. Frank Trainer, a retired machinist from Gainesville, Florida, learned of the fate of this beautiful old machine. He talked the owners into giving it to him, and set it up in his backyard. He restored it mechanically so that it ran like new, but it was beyond his ability to create new animals, restore the woodwork, or re-create the beautiful scenery panels and ceiling murals.

After ten years, Frank's wife, wanting her backyard back, convinced Frank to put this machine up for sale. Betty Burr of Kinsley, Kansas, while surfing the Internet, discovered this carousel frame for sale and convinced the National Foundation for Carnival Heritage of Kinsley to purchase it from Frank. They hired me to carve all new animals representing the masters of the past, and Borislav Peronovich to restore the murals to their former glory. For both Borislav and me, this is much more than just a commission, it is a labor of love. Many of the figures I will show you how to carve in this book are replicas from the old masters I have made for this carousel. The others are creations of my own, made so that one and all, not just the rich, can enjoy carousel art.

In this book, I will introduce you to some of the inspired artists who created carousels, especially in North America, and show you how you can re-create some of their finest works. The life stories of the master carousel carvers from the turn of the twentieth century have inspired and motivated me. They are my mentors, teachers, and friends. I hope they will become yours as well.

There were three main styles of carousel art in the United States: the Philadelphia or "Dentzel" style of carving, the Coney Island, and the County Fair. I examine these styles and their masters in Chapter 1; my own style—essentially a blend of them—will give you ideas to develop your own, in Chapter 2; how to prepare to carve, in Chapter 3; and, in Chapters 4 and 5, how to carve your own carousel animals in miniature and full size.

CHAPTER *1*

&e *Classic Carousels*

The carousel has been around for a longer while than you might suspect and precursors of it were developed independently in several different parts of the world. These early carousels consisted primarily of a center pole with crossbeams attached to a wheel at the top of the pole. Suspended from these crossbeams were seats. These simple contrivances were simply pushed around, usually by a man, but sometimes by an animal—anything from a horse to a dog. Sometimes a pit would be dug under the carousel and planked over, so that the motive power would be "out of sight, out of mind." Illustrations of these early forms of carousel have been found in Europe, the Middle East and India from as early as A.D. 500. When the Spanish conquistadors invaded Mexico, they found the Aztecs playing the game of "flyers." In this game, people would dress up in feathers to look like birds and be suspended from a tall pole by their heels. Ropes hanging from a wheel atop the center pole would then be wound tightly around the center pole. As these ropes unwound, the "bird" people would be flung outward at great speed. This dangerous and sometimes bloody game is played in Mexico even to this day. If you want to see a working model of one of these early forms of carousel, go to a modern day carnival or amusement park and watch the kids having fun on the "Giant Swing"; fortunately, however, the children are not strung up by their heels like the Aztecs, but strapped securely into a seat.

1-1 (FACING PAGE) Elitch Gardens Carousel, Six Flags Amusement Park, Denver, Colorado has been delighting children and adults continuously for more than 75 years. Made and installed in 1925 by the Philadelphia Toboggan Company.

The earliest carousels in the United States and Canada were of this form, made usually by local farmers or blacksmiths to amuse their friends and neighbors at local festivals, as early as the early 1800s. Normally, these early American and Canadian carousels were outfitted simply with chairs, but occasionally an enterprising local would try his hand at creating a simple horse for riders to sit on. These early carousels made in the U.S. and Canada were often called "flying Jennys." You can still see carousels of this sort made by individuals in Central America and Mexico. A friend, Chris Brietenbach, brought me a picture of one he had taken on a recent trip to Guatemala. Intrigued by the idea, together we built a similar machine, which was donated to the National Foundation for Carnival Heritage. It is amazing how popular it is with children and the young at heart. In fact, I have found that it actually appeals more to an older audience than a conventional carousel. As I'm cranking it around by hand, a common call is, "faster . . . faster!" But I get my revenge. I commonly make that individual return the favor by giving me a ride...to my calls of "faster . . . faster!" It's all in good fun.

Origins of the Carousel

The carousel in the form with which we are most familiar probably had its genesis in France about 1680. Someone thought of suspending horses and chariots by chains from arms radiating from a center pole. A man, horse or mule supplied the motive power, and the device was used to train young French nobles for the tournament of ring spearing.

It was in the early 1700s that carousels really started to become popular amusement devices, primarily in France, but to a lesser extent, the rest of Europe as well. The Italians are the ones who gave us the word *carosello*. It referred to a game they played at festivals in which nobles tossed brightly colored perfume-filled balls to each other. The loser was the one who dropped one of these balls, thereby dousing himself with perfume. This is not too unlike the game children play today of tossing water-filled balloons to (or at) each other.

However, it was the French who gave the device today's most commonly used name, "carousel," and added the magic of sitting astride a wooden steed. They also introduced the notion of "catching the brass ring," in which a rider attempts to spear a brass ring as the carousel revolves. Indeed, by the 1820s, the carousel in France was such a common and popular form of entertainment that it was often used by political humorists and cartoonists to express their views.

The French gave us the carousel in the form we are familiar with today, and the rest of the world will be forever indebted to them. But it was the English who provided the innovation and stimulus that propelled the carousel into the modern industrial age.

Introduction of Steam Power

About 1865, S. G. Soams of Marsham, England, tried a steam engine as the motive power in place of a man or horse. The steam engine made the carousel go round and round by use of a flat belt, which wrapped around a drum at the bottom of the center pole. He called it the "Steam Circus," which implies that other animals besides horses were used. It worked, but Soams thought it less than satisfactory, didn't develop it further, and soon abandoned the idea and carousels altogether.

It would not be much of an exaggeration to call Frederick Savage the father of the modern carousel. About 1844, at the age of 16, young Frederick apprenticed himself to Thomas Cooper, who had a small foundry in East Durham. By 1858, he was a master machinist and first exhibited his genius in the form of a road engine at the Long Show.

About 1870, Frederick put together what might be called the first modern carousel, very similarly to the way carousels are made to this day. The way Frederick Savage designed and built his carousels, or "roundabouts" as he called them, allowed for quite large machines. He built three- and four-abreast machines as much as 48 feet in diameter. He also designed the overhead-cranking device, which enables the animals on a carousel to go up and down. Frederick called the animals that went up and down on his carousels "gallopers," a term still used in England today. In the United States and Canada, these figures are known as "jumpers."

Advent of Electricity

About 1911 or 1912, electricity was introduced as the motive power for carousels, bringing carousels to full maturity. Carousels remained extremely profitable until the Depression nearly brought their demise in the 1930s. During World War II, the British government recommended their return and the old machines once again brought joy and happiness. After the war, with the advent of television, the amusement parks in which these old carousels were located became much less popular and less frequently visited. Most of the beautiful old machines were lost to fire, flood, and neglect. The carousels with which most of the post-war generations are familiar are those seen mostly in traveling carnivals, cheap, garish machines, and poorly maintained.

❦ Masters from the Golden Age of the Carousel, circa 1879-1929

While Frederick Savage was perfecting the mechanics of the carousel in England, highly skilled craftsmen and artists, immigrants to America from Europe, were bringing the carousel to its artistic zenith. They transformed the carousel animals, chariots, crestings—indeed the entire carousel—from simple folk art to what can only be considered fine art. Many of these artisans had been employed in Europe by area clergy as sculptors, carving religious icons. They brought the same passion, sensitivity, and level of excellence they had used in the creation of these religious figures to their secular jobs in America as carousel carvers and artists.

These artisans found a freedom in America that stimulated their creativity, with exciting carvings of carousel animals that were imaginative, with florid decoration. This blossoming of design is epitomized in what is termed the "Golden Age" of the carousel, circa 1879 to 1929, during which three predominate styles of carving flourished: the Philadelphia or "Dentzel," the Coney Island, and the County Fair styles.

The Philadelphia or "Dentzel" style is distinguished by realistic-looking animals in natural poses that can usually be identified with master carvers.

Coney Island style is noted for its flamboyance, with wildly exuberant yet generally well-proportioned animals and extravagant decoration of flowers, ribbons, lace, and glass jewels. The distinguished carvers in the Coney Island style did not let anatomical correctness interfere with their exuberance.

The third style, the County Fair style, known more for its manufacturers than its carvers, produced strong, simply carved, functional animals that would hold up under the stress of being moved every few days in traveling carnivals with portable carousels. These animals were often more stylized and, especially early on, primarily folk art in appearance.

Philadelphia or "Dentzel" Style

The Philadelphia or "Dentzel" style of carving is known as such because the companies that produced this style were located in Philadelphia. The best and most successful of them were the Dentzel Company and the Philadelphia Toboggan Company. This style of carving is often referred to simply as the Dentzel style of carving, since the Philadelphia Toboggan Company, or PTC as it is more commonly known, came later and emulated the Dentzel style. In fact, several of the Dentzel carousel company carvers worked for the PTC at one time or another.

The Philadelphia or "Dentzel" style of carving is most notable for the startling realism of the various animals. The phrase that leaps to mind when you see a figure done in the Philadelphia style is "elegant beauty." Figures in this style were created almost exclusively for stationary, park machines.

1-2, 1-3, 1-4 Gustav Dentzel, considered the pioneer American craftsman, started a company in 1867. The Dentzel lion featured in his carousels through the turn of the century.

This is the Kit Carson County Fairground carousel, Burlington, Colorado. Although this carousel was made by the Philadelphia Toboggan Company, circa 1903, the figures were actually carved by Salvatore Cernigliaro, the Muller brothers, and Charles Leopold for the E. Joy Morris Company. The PTC acquired over 200 figures from the E. Joy Morris Company and used them on their first six carousels. All of these carvers worked for the Dentzel factory for most of their careers.

This carousel, considered the premier antique carousel anywhere, was originally shipped to Elitch Gardens (now Six Flags) in Denver, Colorado, in 1905. When Elitch Gardens purchased a new carousel in 1925, this was purchased by Kit Carson County, nearly forgotten and then restored in 1977 by Will Morton and John Pogzela of Denver.

(The photo above left includes Charity White Saddler.)

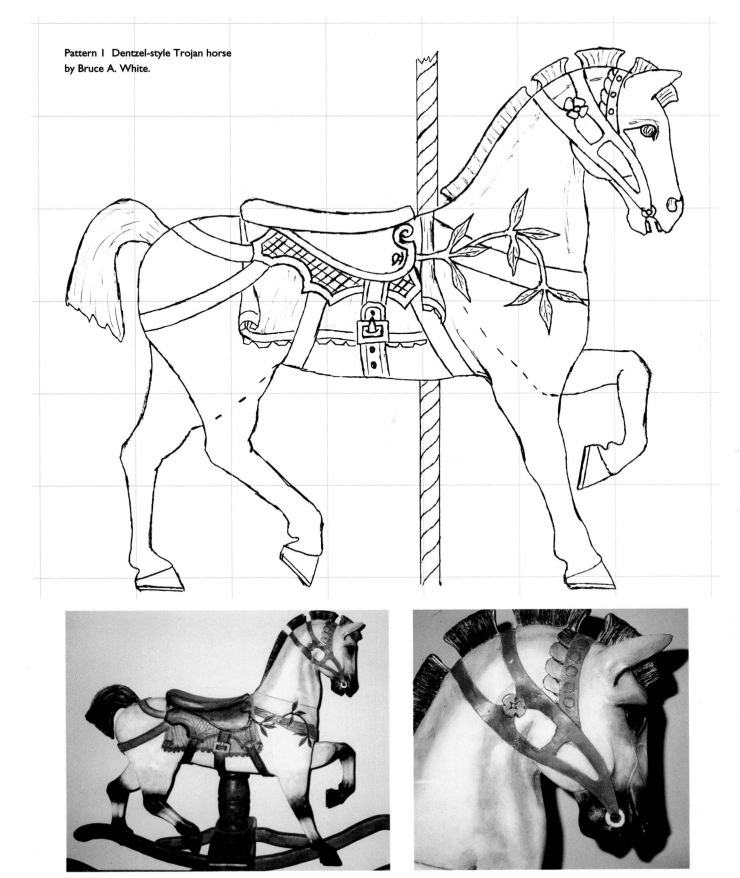

**Pattern 1 Dentzel-style Trojan horse
by Bruce A. White.**

1-5, 1-6 Dentzel-style Trojan horse carved by Bruce A. White.

Pattern 2 Blue Ribbon Betsy, Dentzel-style, by Bruce A. White and Mary Ann Stone.

The Dentzel Family

The Dentzel carousel dynasty began with Michael Dentzel in Kreuynach, Germany, in the 1830s. The animals were very simple and primitive in appearance. His carousels were powered by either a man or a horse, pushing a long lever in a pit under the carousel. Michael's son Gustav learned the trade from his father.

Gustav emigrated to the United States in 1860 at the age of 20, and opened a cabinet shop in Philadelphia. He built his first carousel in 1867, which was a simple affair. It was actually a carousel swing. It had no horses or other animals—just planks suspended by chains on which the riders sat while Gustav pushed the carousel around.

Encouraged by the success of this first machine, Gustav changed the sign on his cabinet shop to read, "G. A. Dentzel, Steam and Horse-power Carousel Builder — 1867," and started construction of his first real carousel.

It was such a success that Gustav dismantled and transported it to be set up as the first carousel at the resort of Atlantic City. Its success inspired Gustav to take the carousel on tour. At a stop in Richmond, Virginia, Gustav learned an important lesson. He couldn't understand why nobody was riding the carousel that had been so successful everywhere else. The local schoolboys were actually throwing rocks at it!

Finally, in exasperation, Gustav protested to a police officer standing idly by. The officer informed him, "If you want people to ride your merry-go-round, you had better change your music." Gustav was playing "Marching Through Georgia" on his band organ. This was shortly after the Civil War, remember, and General Sherman's victorious march through Georgia was not fondly remembered in the South. Gustav quickly changed his music, won them over in Richmond, and never repeated that mistake.

His tour a success, Gustav went into carousel manufacturing with all his heart. And like most of the successful carousel manufacturers, he retained ownership of some of them. In a National Association of Amusement Parks publication of 1938 cited in Frederick Fried's *A Pictorial History of the Carousel* (Vestal Press, Ltd., 1964), Lamarcus A. Thompson describes a visit to a Dentzel carousel in 1876: "Down by the Sands [Hotel?] of Atlantic City, I found a baby in a soapbox. The box was strapped on the side of a horse next to the center pole of a merry-go-round. In the box was little Billy Dentzel. Bill's mother was selling tickets, his father Gustav was taking up the tickets, watering the horses, and looking after the merry-go-round."

By the 1880s, Gustav was using steam power, which enabled him to build larger and more elaborate carousels. With orders pouring in, he built a three-story addition to his shop. However, his profits from the rides he owned far exceeded his income from the manufacture of carousels.

Gustav A. Dentzel died on January 22, 1909. That little boy strapped to the side of the horse pulling his father's carousel—Billy, or "Hobbyhorse Bill" as he was called—took over the business. Bill had worked in the carving shop for

1-7 Blue Ribbon Betsy carousel horse is faithful to the Dentzel style, especially in regard to the realism. The "prancing," or back legs on the platform, front legs reared up, was a common pose used by the Dentzel firm prior to 1900. The flyaway mane was used by the firm occasionally in later years. The owner, Mary Ann Stone, is fond of dogwood flowers and butterflies, thus the decor.

many years and was familiar with all phases of management and production in the business. He made an even greater success of the business than his father. By his death in 1929, he was a millionaire.

The Dentzel family, and Bill in particular, brought the carousel to its highest, most artistic level. Shortly after his death, the stock market crashed and the world entered the Great Depression. In a very real sense, the golden age of the carousel can be said to have died with "Hobbyhorse Bill" Dentzel.

The Muller Brothers

Daniel and Alfred Muller were two exceptionally talented carvers who immigrated to the United States with their family as young boys in 1882. Of the two, Daniel is the more celebrated and more is known about him. Daniel is widely acknowledged as perhaps the best carousel carver ever, with his brother Alfred given hardly a footnote. But having seen some of the work known to have been done by Alfred, I have to wonder if some of his work has not been mistakenly attributed to Daniel. The work identified as Alfred's seems to me every bit as inspired as that attributed to Daniel.

The difference is that Daniel devoted his entire life, body and soul, to his art, carving both for carousels and for its own sake. Alfred did not.

◌ How Things Were Done Way Back When

Writing to an associate as an old man, Daniel Muller, a former carver for Gustav Dentzel, recounts the following story*: "At that time, the carousel had no horses, just seats like park benches, and somebody turned the ride by hand. When I worked in the shop, there was an old book in which there were prints for all types of animals. My father said he traced the horses from the book, took it to be enlarged to working size, cut a pattern, and from the pattern cut the block of wood. Then he carved it to shape."

This account does not quite conform to chronology: records show Daniel's father Johann to have immigrated to the United States from Germany in 1882, but it does show an interesting insight into how things were done. I don't approach the job much differently more than 100 years later.

* Story quoted from a letter from Daniel Muller printed in Frederick Fried's *A Pictorial History of the Carousel* (Vestal Press, Ltd., 1964).

Artistically, he seemed to be content to live in his big brother's shadow. And when the carousel industry crashed with the stock market in 1929, he sought employment in other fields. Daniel, on the other hand, pursued his art with a rare passion to his dying day.

Marcus Illions is quoted as having said of Daniel, "Daniel Muller? Now there is a real artist!" High praise indeed from a man considered in his time to have been the "best," and by many since.

Daniel Muller was born in Hamburg, Germany, in 1872. His father Johann was a close friend of Michael Dentzel (the father of Gustav Dentzel), and quite likely worked for him as a carver. Emboldened by the success of Gustav in America, Johann moved his family to the United States in 1882. They settled in Brooklyn, New York, where it appears that he first worked as a carver for Charles Looff.

In 1888, Johann moved his family to Sunnytown, Pennsylvania, where he and his two sons, Daniel and Alfred, went to work at the Dentzel factory. Both Daniel and Alfred had attended art school, and their knowledge and talent soon became evident. When the boys' father died in 1890, Gustav took them under his wing and treated them like his own sons. Through the 1890s, Daniel continued to study art while he worked as a carousel carver. He often entered and won sculpture competitions.

Gustav Dentzel may have treated the Muller boys as his own, but he was a strict and demanding father figure. Eventually, as young men, they decided to strike out on their own. Around 1899, they hired on with the newly formed Grey Manufacturing Company, the precursor to the PTC. Gustav never forgave the two young men for what he considered their failed loyalty.

One explanation for the brothers' leaving the Dentzel firm is that Daniel, in particular, may have felt that his artistic integrity was being compromised by the Dentzel "system."

Pattern 3 Muller-style "Sir Valentino" horse by Bruce A. White and David Stone.

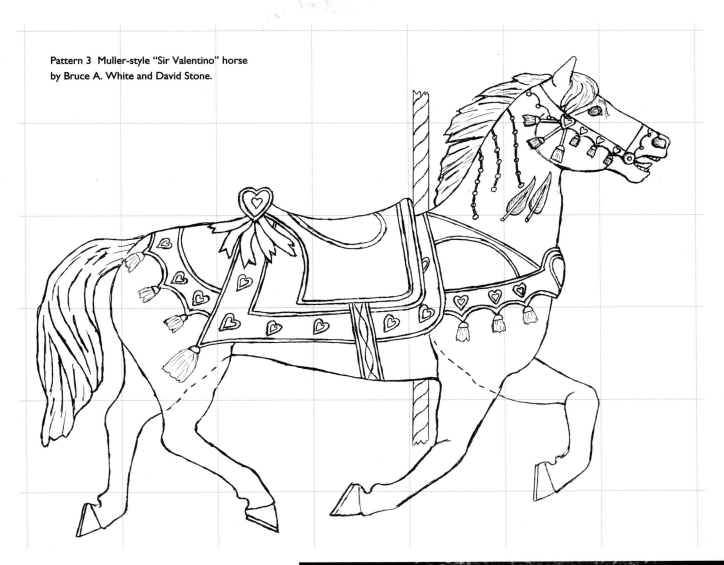

1-8 Muller-style "Sir Valentino" horse, carved by Bruce A. White from Honduran mahogany (*Swietenia macrophylla*) with decoration sculpted in putty, is based on a pattern originated by Daniel or Alfred Muller, originally as an Indian pony in the standing position. The owner, David Stone, redesigned the decor to include the hearts and tassels. Painted by Cindy White.
Carving time: 120 hours.

The Dentzel factory required carvers to work from patterns. Some artistic discretion was allowed, but only within set limits. Daniel was becoming recognized as a fine artist in his own right, having won several national sculpture competitions with his renderings of female nudes. Gustav may have begun experimenting with duplicate-carving machines as early as 1898. This may well have been more of a compromise to his artistic integrity than Daniel was willing to bear.

The work of the Muller brothers was undoubtedly one of the key factors to launching the PTC's long and successful career. They left, however, after only three years, to form their own company, the D. C. Muller and Brother Company, in 1902. It remained in business until 1917. They made a few complete carousels for themselves, which they owned and operated, but primarily provided figures for other companies. The brothers did figures in many styles, but were especially noted for their cavalry horses. Their figures were carved with astonishing detail, going so far as to carve even the stitching in the saddles. Their figures were often compared to the sculptures of Augustus Saint-Goudens. Daniel continued his formal artistic training, attending classes at night. He studied under the noted portrait/bust sculptor, Charles Grafly, for 12 years at the Pennsylvania Academy of Fine Arts.

The Muller brothers may have been exceptional artists, but they were not very good businessmen. Their company never did particularly well financially. When Gustav Dentzel died and his son Bill took over the helm of his father's firm, he extended an offer to the Muller brothers to come back to work for him, which they accepted. They worked for Bill until his death, when the Dentzel Company closed its doors. Daniel went into semi-retirement and repaired and refurbished carousel figures until 1940. He died at the age of 79 in 1951. It is not known what became of his brother Alfred, who lived in his big brother's shadow all his life.

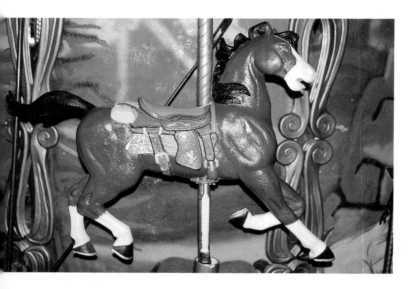

1-9 (Top) "Tex, the Cowboy Horse," three-quarter-size carousel horse casting from the original carved from black walnut (*Juglans nigra*) by Bruce A. White. It closely resembles a design originated by Daniel Muller, circa 1898, shortly before he left the Dentzel firm. Painted by Nancy Klenke.

1-10 "Billy the Muller Goat," original design by Daniel Muller, circa 1907, carved for the Carnival Heritage Carousel, Kinsley, Kansas by Brent White as a memorial for his and Bruce's brother, Steve, from driftwood gathered near Brent's home in Poulsbo, Washington. It is decorated with finely carved bells and the characteristic Muller "Punch" figure on the back of the saddle. Painted by Arinda Jones. Carving time: 120 hours.

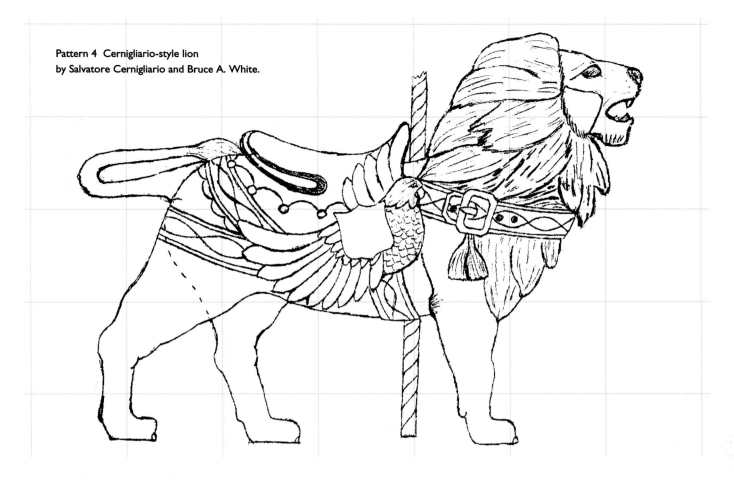

Pattern 4 Cernigliario-style lion
by Salvatore Cernigliario and Bruce A. White.

Salvatore Cernigliaro

Salvatore Cernigliaro, affectionately known as "Cherni," was an immigrant from Sicily who arrived penniless and alone in Philadelphia in October 1902. He had started carving at an early age, apprenticing at age 13 to a noted Italian craftsman. In Italy, he helped decorate churches, palaces, villas, and businesses. Hearing of the opportunities available to enterprising young men in America, he decided to emigrate. He soon found employment with the Dentzel firm (see the sidebar on page 21 with his account "in his own words").

Cherni came with what he called his "box of gold," his box of handmade tools, and he immediately caused an uproar: not understanding the Dentzel "system" or the instructions the other carvers were trying to give him, he just started free-form carving. That very year, 1903, Dentzel had incorporated duplicate-carving machines

into production. Cherni had no idea that the company used patterns—machine cut, roughed-out shapes—that the carvers merely finished. Naturally enough, this upset the other carvers. Fortunately, Gustav recognized Cherni's exceptional artistic skills and allowed him free reign. Cherni, through Gustav's indulgence, revolutionized the Dentzel factory and the carousel industry. It was he who introduced the rabbits, goats, lions, giraffes, and other menagerie figures prized by collectors and soon imitated by the other companies. He also introduced the flowers, drapery, angels, Indians, and other secondary figures (known as "Cherni figures") that other companies soon copied, as well as the Arabian style horse with its sensitive, noble head.

Shortly after the PTC formed, its president, Henry Auchy, wanting to hire the very best carvers, approached Cherni with the offer to "name your own price." Cherni, out of gratitude, loyalty, and

1-11 "Cherni's Lion," carved full size from basswood (*Tilia* spp.) by Bruce A. White for the Carnival Heritage Carousel in Kinsley, Kansas, is faithful to the carving of Salvatore Cernigliaro, circa 1910, except for the mane, inspired by a picture Bruce found in a *National Geographic* magazine of a lion facing into the wind, its mane swept, which he thought was perfect for a carousel. Painted by Charity White Saddler. Carving time: 120 hours.

1-12 Another view of the full-size "Cherni's Lion," carved for the Carnival Heritage Carousel in Kinsley, Kansas.

1-13 "Cherni's Lion," carved in miniature by Bruce A. White for his parents' 50th wedding anniversary. Carving time: 30 hours.

affection for Gustav, turned him down. Gustav is quoted by Cherni as having said of the PTC, "they are like mushrooms, they won't last long." A few years later, Gustav died. When his son Bill died in 1929, the PTC finally got Cherni, and he worked for them until he retired from carousel carving.

Cherni was an exceptionally fast carver. He could take one of the machine cut, roughed-out figures, and finish it in a week or less. By all reports, he was a compassionate and sensitive man. Not wanting to embarrass his coworkers, he often did his work for the Dentzel factory at his home. After Cherni retired from the PTC, he moved to California to be near his daughter Marguerite. He taught sculpture there at an art school until the age of 87. He died in 1974 at the age of 94.

The PTC is still in business today manufacturing carousels, reorganized under the name "Carousel Magic!" out of Mansfield, Ohio. When Carousel Magic! bought out the old PTC inventory and was preparing to open its doors in 1993 as a carving school and manufacturer of carousels, they called me and asked if I would go to work for them as a carver and instructor with an offer similar to that given to Cherni. Like Cherni, I turned them down, desiring instead to pursue my own dream.

✒ "Cherni" in His Own Words

In October 1902, I landed in the United States as immigrant. I was alone and few coins in pocket, 23 years old, healthy and a very, very strong boy full of energy and corragio. I was coming from Palermo, Italy; my trade was wood carver in furniture. The first job I got in Philadelphia was with a Mr. Morris, a wealthy man who manufactured red merry-go-round, not for sale but for his own use, or his own parks. It was a new job for me carving wood horses for merry-go-round as I was carver for furniture. But I didn't get lost. Very quickly I got acquainted with the new work and I like it very much. After three months, summer came, Mr. Morris closed his shop and opened his park so I was out of work. I ask somebody if there was any other carousel shop in Philadelphia. They told me of Mr. Dentzel's shop in Germantown near Erie Avenue.

I managed to find the place. Facing Germantown Avenue was Mr. Dentzel's house where he lived . . . inside a large yard was a little factory. When I entered the yard, Mr. Dentzel was in front of the house and stopped me. That time, I couldn't speak English—only I could say three words—me carver, job? Mr. Dentzel noticed I was an immigrant and talked to me in German, which I couldn't understand. I understood there was no job for me and I walked away. After one week I was still out of work. It happened that I was still around for any job and I found myself near Mr. Dentzel's shop and one block from the shop where is St. Stefano Church. I went into the church and I pray. I said, "Mr. Lord, I have only $4.00 in my pocket—it is my last pay for my board and if I don't find a job now, they will throw me out." It was a hot day and I was very thirsty. I remember that in the middle of the Dentzel yard was an artesian well. When I got there, again Mr. Dentzel was in front of his house. He recognize me and started again to talk in German. Again I repeat my three words, me carver, job?

Mr. Dentzel was a good man and feel pity for poor immigrant, so he motion me to follow him. Inside shop, there was a very good wood carver, Mr. Boory, a Tyrolean, who could speak a few Italian words. He told me that Mr. Dentzel one week ago gave me job but I didn't come. I said I didn't understand him. He told me to bring my tools and start work immediately. I went out of the shop to St. Stefano Church and I thank Lord.

—quoted from a letter from Salvatore Cernigliaro printed in Frederick Fried's *A Pictorial History of the Carousel* (Vestal Press, Ltd., 1964).

The Philadelphia Toboggan Company (PTC)

The Philadelphia Toboggan Company, or the PTC as it is more commonly known, was formed in 1903 and has been in continuous operation to this day, as mentioned above, under one banner or another. Its long-term success can probably be attributed to two important factors: first and most important, it has always been run by people who had already made a success in the business world—not carvers, who are, after all, artists, and we all know what that means. Nearly as important, they have always been concerned with the entire carousel, not just the animals or the mechanical parts. The PTC's goal has always been to create a complete, integrated work of art. The company even designed and built beautiful gazebo-like buildings to house many of its machines and carefully landscaped the grounds around the buildings. They have always endeavored to create a three-minute escape for the child and the child at heart, a waking, magical "dream." They were true "dream weavers."

The co-founder of PTC and driving force behind the company was Henry Auchy. He was born in January of 1861 in Lower Salford, Pennsylvania. He went into the produce business as a young man and soon branched out into the liquor business, which is where he made his fortune. Entranced by the carousels being built in his hometown of Philadelphia, and intrigued by the business opportunities they afforded, he formed the Grey Manufacturing Company in 1899 to build and operate his first carousel, which he placed in a park he owned, Chestnut Hill Park, in Philadelphia. Spurred on by its success, he formed a partnership with Louis Berni (of band organ fame) in 1900 to form the Philadelphia Carousel Company. Berni soon dropped out, however, and the company foundered.

Pattern 5 PTC Jumper
by John Zalar, circa 1922.

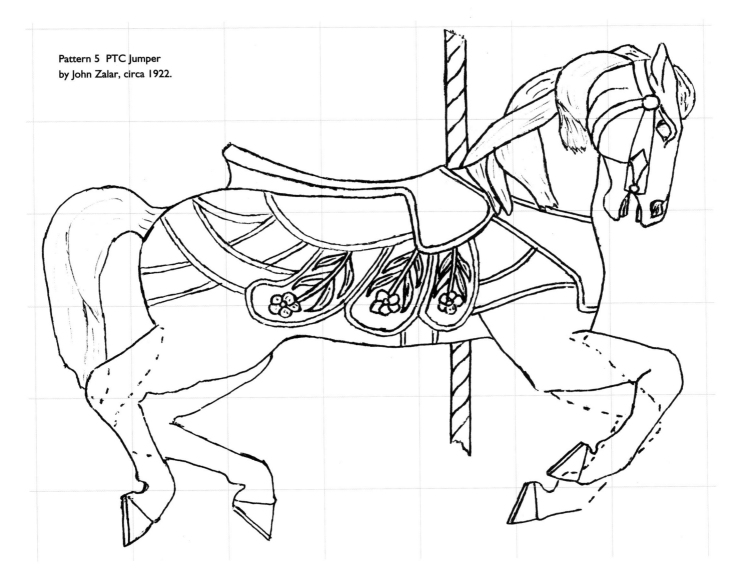

Three years later, in 1903, Henry joined with Chester Albright to form the Philadelphia Toboggan Company, to build carousels and roller coasters. Their stated mission was to "build finer and better carousels and coasters."

Their first move was to buy the roller coaster patents and inventory of over 200 carousel figures from the E. Joy Morris Company. They used these figures to build their first carousels. Some of these figures were done by Cherni before he went to work for the Dentzel firm, but most were done by a man named Charles Leopold. Little is known of Mr. Leopold except that he was a very talented carver and that he also worked for the Dentzel firm as the "head man." At that time, being the "head man" meant just exactly that: he carved the heads for the carousel figures. Since this is the most important and difficult part of a carousel figure to carve, the "head man" was naturally highly respected by the other carvers and the company owners, and he was very often also the factory foreman. So when an apprentice was told to go see the "head man," he was really being sent to see the boss.

The business savvy the partners showed in purchasing these figures from the Morris firm was little short of genius and clearly demonstrates why the PTC has been successful for so many years.

The next move the partners made was to hire the very best carvers to be had. As previously mentioned, Cherni turned them down, but they hit

1-14 PTC Jumper, the No. 1 copy of the first figure Bruce A. White made for Rotocast/Wonder Toys and the carousel horse that Applebee's used in their restaurants until Bruce designed a new one, specifically for them, is a three-quarter version of an original PTC design by John Zalar, circa 1922. Production requirements mandated some modifications, eliminating undercuts and fine detail as well as repositioning of the legs, head, and tail slightly to give the figure the illusion of being larger than it actually is. Painted by Cindy White.

1-15 The head of the original carving from poplar (*Populus alba*) of the PTC jumper. Carving time: 80 hours.

pay dirt with the Muller brothers. With the purchase of the original 200 figures from the Morris firm and the Muller brothers providing them new ones, PTC was now a force to be reckoned with.

From 1903 to 1907, PTC sold carousels as fast as they could make them. The artistic mastery of Daniel and Alfred Muller assured that the figures were elegant and well proportioned. They had elaborate and beautiful decorations. Although Cherni did not work for them, they had a number of his carvings among the 200 figures they had purchased from Morris, and his influence is much in evidence. The PTC figures carved during this period often had secondary figures known in the industry as "Cherni figures," angels, Indians, panthers, and frogs, etc., carved as the saddle pommel or peering out from behind the cantle of the saddle.

In 1907, disaster struck the company. The Muller brothers stopped supplying the PTC to start making their own carousels. From 1907 to

1-16 Elitch Gardens Carousel, Six Flags Amusement Park, Denver, Colorado is the carousel that Elitch Gardens bought when it sold the circa 1903 carousel now found in Burlington, Colorado. This carousel was made by the Philadelphia Toboggan Company in 1925.

1912, the PTC averaged only one carousel per year. The quality declined and the carvings were, for the most part, uninspired.

A man named Leo Zoller was evidently the master carver during this period when, with the exception of a few hippocampus figures (half horse, half fish), only horses were produced. The hippocampus figures were generally quite good, but the horses were often poorly proportioned, with elongated heads, eyes placed too high, and legs awkwardly positioned. Though Zoller's actual carving appears to have been fairly adequate, the composition of his figures is somewhat wanting. It seems his work may have suffered under the

handicap of undue restrictions and guidelines set by management. Just as the Muller brothers left the Dentzel firm, they may have left the PTC to preserve their artistic integrity and standards.

Though the carousel figures may have suffered during this period, the chariots for the carousels reached a level of artistry not seen before or since. The mural paintings, buildings, and landscaping also maintained their level of excellence.

The company was revitalized in 1912 with the hiring of Frank Caretta as the new master carver. They also started obtaining carvings from Charles Carmel, a freelance carver whom I will discuss in a later section.

1-17, 1-18, 1-19 Carousel figures from the Elitch Gardens Carousel, Six Flags Amusement Park, Denver, Colorado shown in 1-16. Made by the Philadelphia Toboggan Company in 1925, most, if not all, of the figures were probably machine-carved from prototypes carved by John Zalar and Frank Caretta. The carvings are elaborate and expressive with the trappings often works of art themselves.

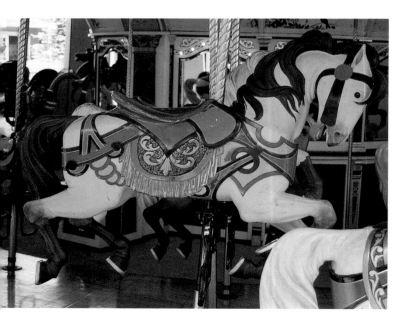

Frank Caretta emigrated to the United States as a youth from Milan, Italy. He learned his trade as a furniture carver in Philadelphia, and eagerly sought work at the PTC when he learned of more interesting opportunities there. He was hired on the spot. Frank found that he had a natural talent for designing and carving horses. Within 12 months, he became the "head man," developing new patterns and revitalizing the ailing company. Not only did he bring back realistic-looking horses, he carved fancy scrollwork, cherubs, and other details for the frame of the machine. He spent nights teaching carving to aspiring artists.

In 1915, the PTC hired another very talented carver, John Zalar, an immigrant from Austria. In Austria, Zalar had made a living sculpting religious figures in plaster, marble, and wood. Before getting a job with I. D. Looff, he made a living in the United States designing ornamental ironwork. Zalar worked first for the Looff Carousel Company in Coney Island, New York, and then in Long Beach, California. His carousel horses, when he worked for the Looff firm, were often characterized by a "tucked" head. He departed the Looff firm in 1915 when his wife Johanna died suddenly, leaving him with six children. He moved back east to Philadelphia to remarry, and found work with the PTC. Five years later, he developed a severe case of tuberculosis and was advised by his doctors to move to a drier, warmer climate. Following his doctor's advice, he moved back to California. However, the PTC so valued his work that they continued to purchase figures from him and ship them to Philadelphia for another three years, until he was too sick to continue work. He died two years later in 1925.

In 1919, Samuel High became associated with the company as a stockholder and a member of the board of directors. He eventually bought out Henry Auchy and Chester Albright.

By 1925, the PTC was no longer making new figures, only refurbishing old ones for its new carousels. Frank Caretta as carver and Gustav Weis as painter were the lone workers kept on to do the carousels. The PTC bought out the Dentzel Company in 1929, following the death of Bill Dentzel. They stopped making carousels altogether in 1933, but they kept Frank Caretta on until the 1940s as a carpenter. As mentioned on page 21, the PTC still operates, reorganized in 1993, under the name "Carousel Magic!" out of Mansfield, Ohio.

PTC Roster of Carvers

The "Who's Who" of the Philadelphia Style of Carving*:

F. H. Bensel	David Lightfoot
T.O. Bradshaw	Otto Melzar
A. Bruss	Robert Morris
Albert Cardenti	Alfred H. Muller
Frank Caretta	Daniel C. Muller
Charles Carmel	Henry Noy
Salvatore Cernigliaro	Henry E. Richard
John Demian	Salvatore Pat Russo
William Eules	Joseph Tornatore
Jose Garlick	Louis Valenti
Jacob Krisavsky	Dan Vecciolli
Vincenzo Lanza	John Zalar
Frank Leon	

Machine Carvers: "Roughed out" with duplicate-carving machines for finish carvers:

Carmine Chiarlanga

Charles J. Lorenz

C. J. Martin

* Source is the PTC list printed in Frederick Fried's *A Pictorial History of the Carousel* (Vestal Press, Ltd., 1964).

Coney Island Style

Named, like the Philadelphia style, for the geographical location in which it was centered, the Coney Island style of carving is most noted for its flamboyance. The figures are commonly very animated, even aggressive in appearance, the manes tossed wildly and the mouths split wide in wild whinnies. The decoration was usually extravagant, with the animals draped in profusions of flowers, ribbons, lace, and other decor. Glass jewels were used in abundance and gold and silver leaf were often features in the manes and tails. The animals were generally well proportioned, but the artists who were the masters of this style did not let anatomical correctness get in the way of the wild exuberance they attempted to portray. More sedate tastes might label this style as "too much" or "over the top," but the success of the manufacturers of figures in this style and the high prices they now bring at the auction block suggest that they were right on target.

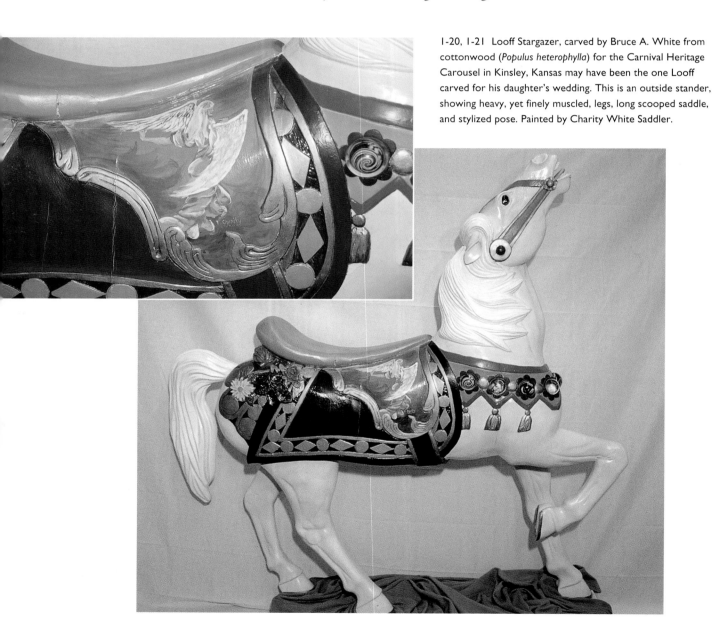

1-20, 1-21 Looff Stargazer, carved by Bruce A. White from cottonwood (*Populus heterophylla*) for the Carnival Heritage Carousel in Kinsley, Kansas may have been the one Looff carved for his daughter's wedding. This is an outside stander, showing heavy, yet finely muscled, legs, long scooped saddle, and stylized pose. Painted by Charity White Saddler.

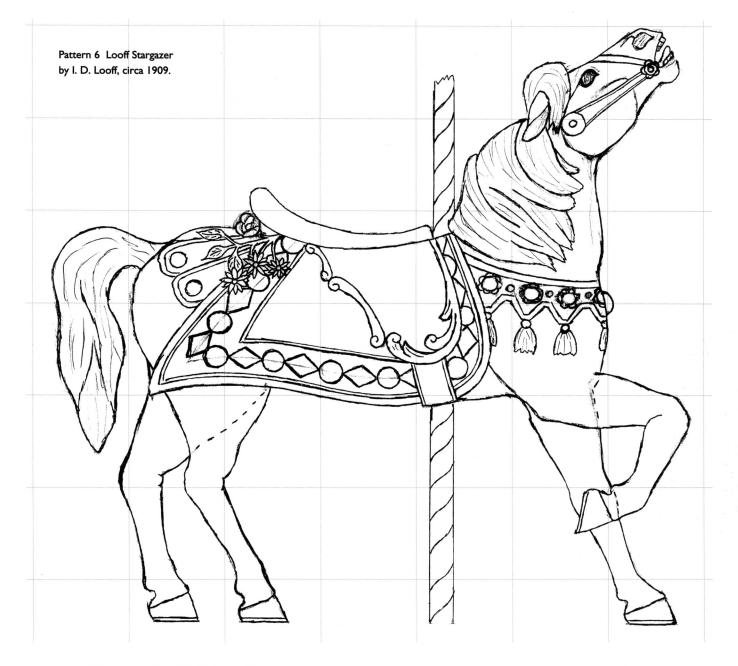

Charles "I. D." Looff

Charles "I. D." Looff was born in Schleswig-Holstein, an often-contested area between Denmark and Germany, in 1852. He emigrated to the United States in 1870, settling in Brooklyn, New York, where he found work as a furniture carver.

Early on, I. D. persuaded the owner of a successful beach pavilion on Coney Island to install a carousel at his resort. I. D. worked alone at night in his basement to make this carousel, single-handedly carving and painting all the animals, murals and trim, and assembling the frame and platform. He embellished the prototype with etched mirrors and other ornamentation, originating what would become known as the Coney Island style. He completed his first carousel in 1876 and it became quite popular and profitable. In 1878, this carousel was sold to a streetcar company. Forty years later, shortly before his death, I. D. sentimentally bought it back.

1-22 An outside figure on the Looff carousel, Spokane, Washington.

1-23 A closed-mouth pony on the Looff carousel, Spokane, Washington. Looff was the only master of the Golden Age of the Carousel who occasionally made his figures with a closed mouth.

I. D. made his second carousel for Charles Feltman (of hot dog fame) for his popular beer garden on Coney Island, where it became a landmark. Young's Pier in Atlantic City, New Jersey, was the site for I. D.'s third carousel. It was so popular that the owner of the pier made a generous offer to I. D. to purchase it. I. D. accepted the offer, and it launched him as a force to be reckoned with in the amusement ride business.

The animals on these first three carousels included a good number of menagerie figures and they had a sweet-faced, folk-art charm to them. I. D. had a lifelong fascination with wild animals: he always kept live, exotic animals and one of his favorite pastimes was visiting zoos. This interest is reflected in the wide and varied use of menagerie animals in his carousel carvings throughout his life.

There was one other carousel I. D. constructed entirely by himself. In 1909, he made a large, very ornate carousel with 52 figures for his daughter Emma's wedding. In fact, this was probably the last carousel for which I. D. carved any figures at all. By this time he was a self-made millionaire and probably needed to devote all his attention and time to the running of his business.

With the seed money from the sale of his Young's Pier carousel, I. D. was able to obtain the service of some very talented carvers. Among them were Marcus Illions, John Zalar, and Charles Carmel. Included among these carvers who were actually more talented than he, was his son, Charles, Jr. Charles designed the chariots and the decorations on the figures for his father's firm and carved most of the company's chariots.

With these carvers, I. D.'s figures lost their early simple charm and became the spirited, flamboyant steeds most commonly associated with the Coney Island style of carving. But while I. D. may not have been the most talented carver in his shop, he had a very keen sense of proportion. He was always a frequent presence in his factory, ensuring that his company made realistic, well-proportioned horses and menagerie figures, regardless of the makeup of his workforce.

I. D.'s patriotic feelings for his adopted country are apparent: he frequently used U. S. flags on his figures and portraits of American heroes and statesmen for the rounding boards. He used equestrian portraits of George Washington as models for his horse poses. He favored secondary carvings under the saddle cantles, such as eagles, cherubs, and lions. He also used "hunter's kill" as subjects. Rabbits, foxes, birds, and other animals were strapped behind the saddle or slung in front of the pommel. The armored carousel horse may have originated with I. D. That his children were fascinated with King Arthur and his court may have been his stimulus. I. D. was always looking for faster, better ways of manufacturing. One of his innovations was the use of molds to make plaster casts of such details as rosettes and tassels, which he attached to his creations.

By 1895, I. D. was making huge carousels. He placed his showpiece at Crescent Park in East Providence, Rhode Island. With 62 animals and 4 chariots, it is one of the most magnificent carousels ever constructed—a celebration of gilt and glitter, cherubs, and neo-Baroque carvings. The influence of Marcus Illions can clearly be seen in this carousel. I. D. also designed and constructed the building that housed it, a magnificent structure replete with stained-glass windows and mirrored panels. He used this carousel as a "floor sample" to show to prospective clients. They would choose the figures they wanted for their own carousels from this one. As business prospered, I. D. branched out into the production of other amusement devices, such as fun houses, scenic railways, roller coasters, and other thrill rides.

I. D.'s Brooklyn property, including his factory, was condemned in 1905 by the city of New York so that they could build a park. He moved his entire operation to Riverside, Rhode Island, to be near his showpiece carousel at Crescent Park. He remained there until 1909, when he moved his

1-24 The world-famous Looff "sneaky" tiger, located on the Looff carousel in Spokane, Washington.

entire operation to Long Beach, California. He made a showpiece carousel there similar to the one in Rhode Island.

On the West Coast, I. D. built a number of amusement parks, including locations in Santa Cruz, Long Beach, and Santa Monica, California, as well as Seattle, Washington. He often made the pavilions covering his carousels large enough to line the perimeter with rows of rocking chairs, so that patrons of his amusement parks could have a shady respite out of the sun. What a delight it must have been on a hot day to relax in a rocking chair and watch the children joyfully ride the carousel.

I. D. Looff built approximately 40 carousels in his lifetime. He died in 1918 at the age of 66 . . . a true rags to riches, "American dream" success story.

Marcus Illions

Born in Vilna, Lithuania, in 1865 or 1866, Marcus Illions was apprenticed at the tender age of seven to a cabinet and carving shop. Very little is known of his early training, but it surely included an education in classical art and Greek and Roman sculpture, as well as training in drawing and draftsmanship, as he was a superb draftsman.

Marcus ran away from home at the age of 14, living briefly in Germany. He then settling in England, where he worked for Frederick Savage. There he carved show wagons, circus wagons, and carousel figures for the roundabouts Mr. Savage constructed.

At the age of 23, Marcus came to America under the employ of the English showman Frank Bostok, in which his first task was finishing an order Mr. Bostok had placed with Mr. Savage for a number of circus show wagons.

Illions and Bostok parted company in 1892 and Illions opened a shop in Brooklyn as a freelance carver, primarily of circus and carousel figures. Despite a reputation as one of the premier carvers in the area, he hated the tedium of running a business, and the business consequently failed. However, even as his business was failing, he continued to supply I. D. Looff, including the figures for Looff's showpiece carousel at Crescent Park, in East Providence, Rhode Island.

Around 1900, Illions went to work for another carousel manufacturer, William Mangels. His job was to restore an early Looff creation, the Feltman carousel, built in 1880. The carousel had nearly been destroyed by fire, and only a few of the figures carved by Looff himself remained. Marcus carved new figures for it and the renovated Feltman carousel became a sensation, one of the most popular and visited carousels in the country. This was the making of Illions' national reputation.

✒ Epitome of Coney Island Style

It was Marcus Illions who introduced the stylized manes and energetic poses that helped establish and came to distinguish the flamboyant Coney Island style.

Marcus Illions was most successful when he was able to concentrate on the creative and artistic side of his business. With the aid of his sons, he was able to do this, and he became a creative whirlwind. He was a true innovator. When other companies started copying his work, it merely challenged him to develop new patterns and styles. He especially liked to experiment with the appearance of motion. Just a few blocks from his home was a racetrack where he watched the races of spirited 2- to 3-year-old thoroughbreds. He sought to capture in his carvings the explosive energy and motion of these colts as they burst from the starting gates.

Marcus was a proud, temperamental, and sometimes moody man. These traits were often reflected in his work; and being the free-spirited innovator he was, Marcus didn't always follow convention. For example, it wasn't customary for a carver to sign his work. Marcus often did, very prominently on what he thought was his better work. He even went so far as to carve his self-portrait as part of the decorations. Also, carousel figures never had a sex. That is, unless you happened to be a client Marcus Illions did not like. Then you were likely to get a mare or stallion as the lead figure on your carousel.

After carving figures for a few more carousels for Mr. Mangels, Illions returned to freelance. This time, however, he had some help: his very talented sons. Harry and Phillip helped carve, Rudy specialized in the mechanical parts, and Barney painted. Perhaps one of the strongest assets of this new company, "M. C. Illions & Sons Carousel Works," was son Phillip. Phillip ably took care of the business details his father found so tedious. With a cooperative team, the new business prospered.

Pattern 7 Illions-style flower horse
by Marcus Illions and Bruce A. White.

The family continued in business from 1909 to 1929. During this time, they made 15 large park machines and 5 or 6 smaller, portable machines. They also made show wagons, ticket booths, scenic coasters, furniture, organ fronts, and church icons.

Since M. C. Illions & Sons never used carving machines, each of the figures Marcus carved was unique. Never a gentle, sweet-faced animal rested in his stable; he kept only spirited, wild-eyed, barely tamed horses, straining for the winner's circle. Since Marcus owned and showed his own live horses, he was able to use them as models too, imparting a studied realism with every stroke of his chisel.

The decorations on his animals were lavish, replete with deep relief carving and lots of glass jewels. His horses usually had thick, billowing manes, often tossed wildly or cascading down to the saddle. Marcus used gold leaf on most of his figures; the manes and tails often had sections flattened to facilitate its application. Though he probably originated the idea, it was quickly copied by other companies.

Following is a sampling of some of the best Coney Island style carousels listed by maker and date of origin, and including where you can find them. The Coney Island style of carving, noted for its flamboyance and wild exuberance, might be thought of as "too much," but the success of the manufacturers of figures in this style suggest that they were right on target. See the related sidebars for a sampling of Philadelphia or "Dentzel" style (page 22) and County Fair style (page 45) carousels. Also consult the Internet site: http://www.carousels.com/mgrlist.htm for a list by state, including Canada, of operating classic carousels.

Carmel/Looff/Stein & Goldstein, circa 1893, Lake Compounce Park, Bristol, CT.

Carmel/Looff, circa 1911, Lighthouse Point Park, New Haven, CT.

Illions, circa 1918, Geauga Lake, Aurora, OH.

Illions, circa 1926, Rye Playland, Rye, NY.

Looff, circa 1895, Whalom Park, Lunenberg, MA.

Looff, circa 1895, Crescent Park, East Providence, RI.

Looff, circa 1904, near Moscone Center, San Francisco, CA.

Looff, circa 1909, Riverfront Park, Spokane, WA.

Looff, circa 1911, Santa Cruz Beach Boardwalk, Santa Cruz, CA.

Looff, circa 1912, Heritage Plantation, Sandwich, MA.

Looff/Stein & Goldstein/Dentzel, circa 1920, Disneyland, Anaheim, CA.

Mangels/Illions, circa 1909, Riverside Park, Agawam, MA.

Mangels/Carmel, circa 1914, Prospect Park, Brooklyn, NY.

Mangels/Carmel, circa 1928, Rye Playland, Rye, NY.

Mangels/Carmel, Coney Island, Brooklyn, NY.

Stein & Goldstein, circa 1908, Central Park, New York, NY.

Stein & Goldstein, circa 1910, Knoebels Amusement Resort, Elysburg, PA.

Stein & Goldstein (outer rows), Parker (inner rows), circa 1911, Pueblo City Park, Pueblo, CO.

Stein & Goldstein, circa 1914, Bushnell Park, Hartford, CT.

Marcus was an extremely fast carver who could carve equally well with either hand. He disdained and ridiculed the use of carving machines, but that did not keep him from employing power tools. He used the band saw like a true virtuoso, in ways in which it was never intended to be used. He often strained the blade beyond its capacity by using it to do most of the rough shaping. Early on, when M. C. Illions & Sons was first getting started, he had a last-minute rush order for a racing derby. Conventional methods would not allow him to complete it by deadline, so son Rudy came to the rescue. Rudy took an old air-powered caulking gun cast off from a nearby shipyard and adapted it so that large chisels and gouges could be attached to it. From then on, Marcus and his pneumatic chisel were inseparable.

Attention to detail characterized all of Marcus' work and the way his shop was run. The "Old Gent" as his sons called him, had a way of "popping up" frequently to check over their work. He supervised every bit of the work from the cutting and gluing up to the final stroke of the paintbrush. He often ran over budget on projects, but was uncompromising on quality. He refused to deliver a less than perfect carousel.

Illions was forced to close his shop in the late 1920s as the use of mass-produced carousel figures increased. His sons scattered across the country to find employment in other amusement businesses. When the stock market crashed, bad real estate investments caused Illions to lose everything. Thereafter, he eked out a living repairing carousel figures and carving religious figures.

I. D. Looff, who died a millionaire and could attribute much of his success to the creative genius of Marcus Illions, is quoted as having said of him, "Mike Illions is the kingpin of the horse carvers."

Illions died impoverished in 1949 at the age of 84. His grave is marked by a simple, uncarved stone.

1-25, 1-26 Illions-style flower horse, carved by Bruce A. White for the Carnival Heritage Carousel in Kinsley, Kansas is faithful to the original configuration by Illions, circa 1909, but Bruce reproportioned the stallion to make it more anatomically correct and softened the look of the face. The number and positioning of the flowers is the same as by Illions, but the sweet pea and other flowers were requested by the Frame family, who sponsored the carving. Painted by Charity White Saddler. Carving time: 240 hours.

Stein & Goldstein

Solomon Stein was born in Russia in 1882 and emigrated to America in 1903 at the age of 21. He settled in Brooklyn, New York.

Just one year earlier, Harry Mandel had arrived in the United States from Russia, speaking not a word of English. Unable to communicate his name to the immigration officials, they dubbed him "Harry Goldstein." He too settled in Brooklyn with his wife and son, and immediately started taking English classes.

These two men said they came to America because "the streets were paved with gold and one could walk free and equal, with no fear of pogroms." If they had to endure hard work and long hours, at least they were confident that it could eventually pay off—sometimes very well. They learned soon enough that their new country was not without its prejudices, though not as extreme as those of their native land. "If you walked in groups, the Marcy Avenue hoodlums wouldn't harm you."

Both men probably learned their carving trade in Russia. Solomon found a job at the Wanamaker Department Store, carving furniture. He free-lanced at night filling carving orders. He quickly settled into life in America, met a fellow Russian immigrant, Anna Goldberg, married her, and had three children.

Harry also quickly found employment, carving small, intricate lady's hair combs. He continued night school, polishing his English. In 1904, he took a job as a carver of models for a mold maker.

Solomon Stein and Harry Goldstein met when they both answered an ad calling for carvers for the Mangels Carousel Works in 1905. They worked for the Mangels Carousel Works under the guidance of Marcus Illions from 1905 to 1907. From Illions they learned much, and their early figures were greatly influenced by him. The two

✎ The Largest Carousel Horses

Stein & Goldstein carved by far the largest carousel horses of their kind. The outside row horses were often life-sized. Their horses typically had elongated muscular bodies and short legs drawn up close to the body if they were jumpers. The heads were modeled after draft horses with long, Roman noses, rather than the refined features of the Arabians and thoroughbreds used by other carvers. The manes were usually thin and wispy. They typically used real horsehair for tails, but most of these were replaced with wooden tails as the original tails became threadbare from children pulling on them.

took great pride in the success and reputation their countryman, Illions, was building for himself, and thought that perhaps they could emulate his success. For his part, Harry felt that, "a comb is smaller and harder to carve than a carousel horse." They left the Mangels factory and went freelance, providing carousel figures for the other carousel companies. When they left the Mangels factory, they may have taken patterns developed by Illions, although this suspicion has not been proven.

They had their first shop in two poorly lit rooms at the end of a long corridor in a crowded tenement. One can only wonder what the other residents thought of their noisy neighbors hammering away with mallet and chisel, late into the night, and the reaction they would receive as they wrestled their wooden steeds down that long corridor for delivery to the various carousel companies.

Stein and Goldstein were not only gifted carvers, but astute businessmen. They realized that the path leading to those "streets paved with gold" was not in carving carousel horses, but in owning and operating the carousels. In 1912, they met Henry Dorber and formed a business relationship

Pattern 8 Parade horse by Solomon Stein and Harry Goldstein, circa 1912. This is the pattern used to carve a carousel horse in miniature in Chapter 4 and full size in Chapter 5.

in which Henry would make the mechanical works while they carved the horses and all the other woodwork.

With the addition of Dorber to their partnership, they were able to move out of their crowded tenement shop to a partially converted stable. It was here that they really started developing their own style. Huge draft horses were still stabled here, and they used them as models rather than the Arabians, Morgans, and thoroughbreds favored by other carousel artists.

The three partners began installing their first carousel at Virginia Beach, Virginia, but it caught fire while being installed. The loss was total. Solomon Stein, who was in Virginia supervising the installation, returned to Brooklyn with only a souvenir disk. He often referred to it as his $20,000 plate.

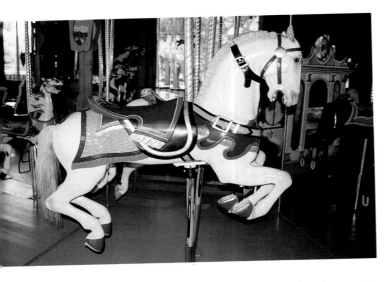

I-27, I-28, I-29, I-30, I-31 (Left and opposite) Pueblo City Park Carousel, Pueblo, Colorado was originally made in 1911 by the C. W. Parker Company of Abilene, Kansas, but the outer row of horses was done by Stein & Goldstein, circa 1907. These two carvers' work was known for the aggressive expressions, bared teeth, laid-back ears, and oversized buckles and saddles. When the carousel was returned to the Parker factory in 1914, these figures were added as the outer row. They probably were made originally as inner row horses for a Stein & Goldstein carousel.

This mixing of carousel figures from different factories was a common practice when figures were lost or damaged or an entire machine was refurbished. All 36 figures on this carousel are shod with iron horseshoes with the Parker, Leavenworth factory logo of "11 Worth."

The loss of this first carousel was financially devastating to the partners, but not fatal. They managed to scrape enough funds together to make a second carousel, which they placed in Brockton, Massachusetts. It was an immediate success. It freed the partners from their financial difficulties and launched the company.

With the success of their second carousel, the partners moved their operation to a converted trolley barn. Their children remember it as being extremely neat and orderly. They loved the aroma of hot glue and fresh sawn wood. Solomon and Harry worked from dawn to dusk, carving all the horses themselves.

Harry was restless at his carver's bench, rocking back and forth as he carved away. Solomon, on the other hand, was very quiet. He worked quickly and with authority. Solomon was said to be intellectually curious, industrious, and innovative—but most importantly—a man who loved people.

Stein and Goldstein never made any menagerie animals, only horses. They continued to use the huge draft horses they knew from their stable days. They carved all the animals themselves, leaving the chariots, mirror frames, and intricate fretwork to others, whom they hired away from the comb factories. They never had more than, perhaps, six people working for them at any one time.

Henry Dorber left the partnership in 1914, but continued to operate one of the carousels. Solomon and Harry reorganized under the title of "Stein and Goldstein, Artistic Carousel Manufacturer" and went on to produce, perhaps, the largest carousels ever made—giant machines to stable their enormous creations, platforms as much as 60 feet across with five and even six animals in a row. With Dorber no longer in the partnership, they obtained the frames for their machines from Mangels, Borelli, Dolle, or Murphy. These giant carousels could seat as many as 100 people.

And they lived up to their claim of "artistic" carousel manufacturers. While they carved the horses, their former comb-carving compatriots produced rims, mirror frames, chariots, and other decorative woodwork of the greatest intricacy and delicacy.

Harry and Solomon did less carving as they became more involved in the operation of their carousels. As the business for new carousels declined, they branched out into buying, selling, and operating other amusement devices. In the early 1920s, they carved circus figures and small barbershop horses for children.

Solomon Stein died of cancer in 1937 at the age of 55. Harry continued to operate two amusement parks until his death at age 80 in 1945.

⚖ *Daring to Dream Big*

Solomon Stein and Harry Goldstein found that if you dare, and if you dream big and work hard, you can walk those "streets paved with gold."

There was nothing sweet or gentle in the appearance of their horses. They always had an aggressive stance. The faces had an air of nervous agitation with their high-set, wild-looking eyes, laid-back ears, and mouths split wide in shrill whinnies. In fact, their horses were often a little bit scary looking. They had definitely broken free of the influence of Marcus Illions and found their own style. To temper the aggressive look of their horses, they nearly always wore garlands of flowers; usually big, deeply carved cabbage roses. Their figures commonly had fish scales and tassels—and always, the Stein & Goldstein trademark, an oversized belt buckle.

Stein & Goldstein undoubtedly made the best armored horses in the business. Perhaps this is because the draft horses they used as models could more naturally carry the heavy armor carved onto them. The lead horse on their carousels was almost always an armored horse.

Charles Carmel

Charles Carmel was born in Russia in 1865, emigrating to the United States in 1883 with his new bride, Hannah, when he was 17 and she 16. They settled into a house with a small, attached shop on Ocean Parkway in Brooklyn, near Prospect Park, where they raised four children and both lived until the day they died.

Virtually nothing is known of his early life or training. It is not known whether he learned the trade of carving in Russia or after his arrival in America. His earlier figures were often sadly disproportionate and unsophisticated in appearance. The heads, especially, of his early figures lacked refinement, being almost cartoonish in appearance, with bulging, poorly placed eyes and "trumpet" noses.

But Carmel was a very apt, if possibly self-taught, pupil. By 1910, he was creating perhaps the ideal carousel horse, achieving a nearly perfect blend of fantasy and realism. He may not have had the grasp of anatomy or proportion that Muller, Looff, or Illions possessed, but this in no way diminished the appeal or charm of his figures.

Carmel always worked as a freelance carver from his shop on Ocean Parkway. He learned so well from the masters of his art, and from his peers in New York and Philadelphia that it is sometimes difficult to tell if a chariot attributed to him is his or one done by Marcus Illions—or if the sea dragon is his innovation, copied by I. D. Looff, or the other way around. Carmel was liable to employ any style. Manes could be tossed wildly like an Illions or a Looff, or be more demure like a Dentzel or a PTC. You could find the military precision of a Muller figure or one of the giant belt buckles so favored by Stein & Goldstein. But one thing was definitely his own: once he got the hang of it, he made the most beautiful, sweet-faced heads of any carver.

✺ Supplier to the Industry

The list of people Charles Carmel supplied carousel animals (or body parts) reads like a Who's Who of the carousel industry. Among them were I. D. Looff, Marcus Illions, Stein & Goldstein, the Muller brothers, the PTC, Mangels, Frederick Dolle, and M. D. Borelli.

His primary client from 1900 to 1905 was I. D. Looff. From 1907 to 1913, Carmel carved three complete carousels for Looff's brother-in-law, Frederick Dolle. Carmel supplied figures for the PTC from 1913 to 1921.

Carmel was the favorite carver for the carousel manufacturer M. D. Borelli, but they did not always see eye to eye artistically. Carmel did not like glass jewels, and used them only sparingly. Borelli, on the other hand, loved them. He would use the winter months to encrust Charles' carvings with glass jewels . . . sometimes as many as 300 on a single figure. Borelli's enthusiastic embellishment sometimes nearly obliterated the detail Carmel had so painstakingly carved.

Carmel may not have always gotten his proportions right, but his realism rang true. He sometimes gave his figures bad teeth and he often employed the drooping tongue he saw on the overworked draft animals passing before his shop. His horses often had strong, aggressive poses, but they were always tempered by the sweet, gentle expressions that were his calling card. He carved very intricate manes, which often had an interesting reverse to their flow at some point. He favored the "stargazer" pose, and the "hunter kill," probably borrowed from Looff. The armored horse was one of his favorite subjects. He loved to embellish his figures with feathers and fish scales.

In 1911, at the age of 45, Charles Carmel succeeded in fulfilling a lifelong dream—he made a

Pattern 9 Armored stander by Charles Carmel, circa 1915. Carmel's horses are known for their nearly perfect blend of realism and fantasy, with a characteristic lolling tongue found on nearly all of his creations. This is one of the finest carousel animals from his later work, which progressed through the years.

carousel of his own. He installed it at Dreamland Park on Coney Island. Then disaster struck the Carmel family.

The night before the carousel was to open, a careless workman knocked over a hot tar pot and the entire park, including Charles' carousel, burned to the ground. Charles had sunk every penny he had into this carousel, and it was not insured. The loss was a crippling blow from which he never recovered. He was never able to make another carousel for himself.

Suffering from arthritis and diabetes, Carmel was able to carve only a few hours a day from then until about 1925. After that, he was completely disabled. He died of cancer in 1931 at the age of 66. Hannah continued to live in that same house on Ocean Parkway until her death in 1946.

Innovator or mimic—does it really matter? Carmel's beautiful figures have brought joy to millions. With their splendid blend of drama and gentleness, realism and fantasy, his just may have been the perfect carousel animals.

County Fair Style

The Philadelphia and Coney Island carvers filled an important niche in the American amusement industry, placing their breathtaking creations at resorts, parks, and trolley car terminals across the United States and Canada. But there was another huge niche that needed to be filled: that of portable carousels, suitable for county fairs and traveling carnivals.

When most people think of carousel animals, this is the style they envision. You didn't have to travel to a resort or one of the large cities to see these dream weavers. They came right to you. In whatever small town or rural area you might be, the traveling carnivals brought you this little bit of magic at least once a year, or more if you were lucky. It was an escape from your daily toil. The personalities and companies that produced these traveling carousels are no less fascinating than those behind the Coney Island and Philadelphia lines.

Charles W. Dare

Not a great deal is known about Charles Dare, but he may have made his first carousel as early as 1867. By 1870, he was operating out of New York City as the "N.Y. Carousel Manufacturing Company," where he worked until 1890. In that year, he moved his factory to Brooklyn, to within a stone's throw of I. D. Looff's factory, and changed the name to "Charles W. Dare Company." He made carousels and other amusement devices there until 1898. He sometimes employed as many as 25 carvers. He died in 1901.

His carousels and their creatures may not have been nearly as fancy as those turned out down the block by I. D. Looff, but they were made for a different market. And they did have a simple, folk-art charm. He had started out as a manufacturer of

By Far the Most Familiar Carousels

Over 80 percent of all carousels made were of the County Fair type. This style of carousel animal was generally smaller and not as ornate. It was designed to be moved every few days. These animals were often more stylized and, especially early on, primarily folk art in appearance. But this does not detract from their charm. Eventually, they achieved nearly the level of excellence of the Philadelphia and Coney Island manufacturers, especially the work of the Herschell-Spillman and Spillman Engineering firms.

Antique County Fair style figures generally bring less at auction than other styles, but sometimes more.

hobbyhorses, and Dare simply used the pattern that had brought him success in that venture.

He had one style of horse and never varied from it, even in the decorations. He just changed the paint scheme. Later on, his horses were slightly refined by the famous carver of cigar store Indians, Samuel Robb, but they kept their simple charm.

His horses had a static pose without the embellishment of muscles and sinew the Philadelphia and Coney Island artists carved into their mounts. The faces were innocent and plump, squeezed into tight halters, with flat nostrils and grinning mouths. Early on, he used real horsehair for the manes as he had for his hobbyhorses, but soon discovered they didn't last long and switched to a very simple, flat mane. He continued to use real horsehair for the tails but, in later years, carousel owners usually replaced these with wood. The saddles too were very simple and sometimes carved separately, so that they could be removed and replaced as needed. The decoration consisted of a simple blanket with a chest strap. For eyes, he used marbles—sometimes clear, sometimes swirled.

Pattern 10 Dare-style "Flag Horse" by Bruce A. White.

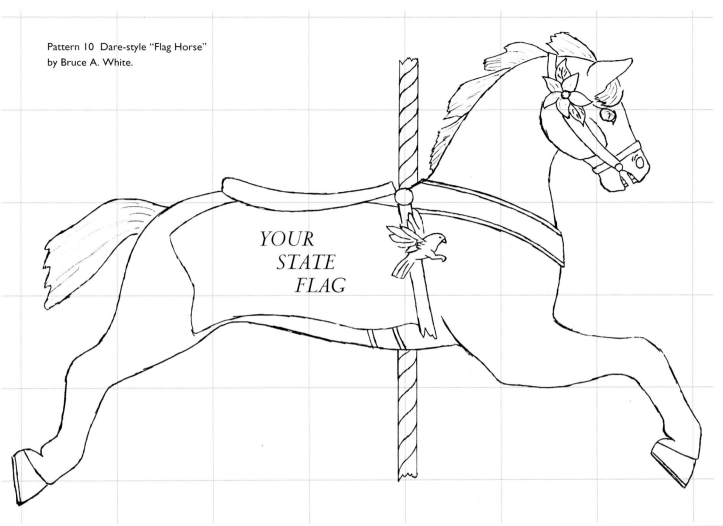

YOUR
STATE
FLAG

1-32 Dare-style "Flag Horse," carved from cottonwood (*Populus heterophylla*) by Bruce A. White for the Carnival Heritage Carousel in Kinsley, Kansas, is based on an original design by an unknown folk artist for the Dare Company, circa 1880.

The Dare Company, perhaps the earliest manufacturer in the U.S., did not use state flags or flowers on the halter, but Bruce wanted to dress it up a bit while still faithful to the Dare style. Dare's simple, primitive designs became emblematic of County Fair style. It has swirled glass marbles for eyes and real horsehair for the tail as the Dare factory used. Painted by Charity White Saddler. Carving time: 40 hours.

Dare also made a wide variety of menagerie animals, including a lion, deer, zebra, goat, camel, donkey, and elephant. As with the horses, they were all carved from the same pattern, always alike, very simple, with that same naive charm.

His chariots were also very simple—basically an unadorned, two-seated gondola suspended from the rafter by chains.

Dare made two types of carousels: the "Flying Horse" carousel, also known as "Flying Jennys" and the "Steam Riding Galleries." Since his machines were made before the introduction of the overhead rocker arms that enabled the animals to go up and down, his Steam Riding Galleries figures were placed on simple mechanisms that allowed riders to bounce up and down on them. The platforms turned on tracks with wheels underneath them.

Charles Dare's carousel figures may have been simple and what could only be termed folk art, but he set the standard and established the mold from which other manufacturers of the County Fair style of carousel did not vary for many years.

◆ A Traveling Carnival Family—

How Kinsley, Kansas Became a Historic Site for American Carousels

About 1901, Charles Brodbeck, a farmer in western Kansas near the small town of Kinsley, took his family to the "Old Settlers Picnic" in Hutchinson, Kansas. Along with the picnic, ballgames, and three-legged races, there was a primitive, wheezing old steam-driven carousel. Charles was amazed at how the farmers and cowboys, after having ridden real horses into town, would put their nickels down to ride a wooden pony in a circle. It got him thinking. About halfway home (80 miles—a four-day journey in those days), he announced to his family, "I think I've found a better way to make a living than farming." He sold some land, hitched up his mules, and returned to Hutchinson to buy that old carousel.

Charles didn't do much with it the first couple of years; he just set it up on his farm and gave rides to the locals. The next summer, however, his son, Fred, persuaded him to let him take it on the road. His first stop was to be the settlers' picnic in Larned, Kansas, 25 miles away, but he got mired in mud about halfway there. He was hungry, dirty, and had no food for his mules. In desperation, he went to a banker in Larned and begged him for enough money to hire some men to get his wagon unstuck and a little besides to tide him over until they could make some money from the carousel. The banker obliged him, against his better judgment. Fred got his dad's carousel set up in time for the picnic and repaid that banker in a matter of hours.

Excited over their success, the Brodbeck sons, Ben and Fred, talked their dad into letting them take his carousel on a circuit of the small towns in Kansas. Charles consented but urged them in future to use the train. Their first stop was Ashland, then Medicine Lodge, then Pratt, where they ran into trouble again. Some local ruffians planned to rob the enterprising brothers but another, more kind-hearted townsman gave them warning. Fred and Ben were ready when the ruffians came and greeted them with birdshot. The reputation they established then prevented any further such attempts. The brothers did so well with their first summer road tour that their father chose to quit farming and join the show. With profits from the show, he was soon able to buy a Ferris wheel.

The Brodbeck family operated carnivals out of Kinsley for the next 70 years, adding rides and attractions yearly. By the 1950s, they may have been the largest family-owned carnival in the country, with a reputation as one of the cleanest, most honest operations in the business. And the backbone of their show was always the carousel. The rigors of the road soon made it necessary to replace that first carousel, and they went through half a dozen more over the years.

Allan Herschell and His Companies

As a purveyor of joy to the masses, one man stands head and shoulders above the rest. He may not have been given the title of "Hobbyhorse King," in fact his passing earned hardly a footnote. But he and his companies brought the magic of carousels to every nook and cranny of the United States and to every corner of the world. You didn't have to live in a large urban center to enjoy his companies' creations; they were brought right to your hometown by the traveling carnivals. They were brought to you over 100 years ago, and they are still brought to you today. His carousels may not have been as fancy, ornate, or realistic as those made by the Philadelphia or Coney Island companies, but ask just about anyone, anywhere, about the more magical moments of their childhood, and they will probably mention when the carnival came to town and they had their first ride on a merry-go-round. Most of these took place on a carousel made by Allan Herschell or one of his companies.

Allan Herschell was born poor in 1851 in Arbreath, Forfarshire, Scotland, one of 13 children. He apprenticed himself at a young age to the machinist and mold-making trade. He emigrated to the United States with his parents at the age of 19, settling first in Buffalo, where he took work as a foundry foreman. The company he first worked for was failing from the start and soon went out of business. With James Armitage, whom he met while working for this company, Herschell pooled his resources to buy their former employer's equipment and start their own company. They moved their fledgling business in 1873 to North Tonawanda, New York, and called themselves the North Tonowanda Engine & Machine Company. After two fires in their first year of operation, the second in which they lost nearly everything, they reorganized as the Armitage-Herschell Company. Allan's brother, George, soon joined the partnership. The company made primarily steam engines, boilers, mill and agricultural equipment. With the reorganization and the addition of brother George as treasurer, the company was soon very successful, with orders pouring in.

Allan suffered from ague his entire life. While on a train trip to New York City in 1883 to consult with yet another doctor, he chanced to see a portable carousel made by Charles Dare and he was captivated by it. He tried to persuade his partners to make one, but business was good and they saw no reason to take the risk. But Allan made one anyway, over his partners' objections, using company assets and employees. It did fairly well, and he soon sold it. He then made and sold another. In 1885 he made a third carousel, still very much with his partners' objections. He took it to the World Exposition & Cotton Centennial in New Orleans for three months to see if he could market it, as recounted in the box below.

The carousel may have generated "smoke and fumes," but it also made a lot of money. And orders. Allan returned from New Orleans with a fist full of orders and his partners finally decided, grudgingly, to go along with Allan and add carousels to their line of products. It was the smartest move they ever made. The partners were soon employing over 100 people full time and shipping out an astonishing number of carousels— by 1891, nearly 100 a year. By 1894, an almost unbelievable 300 carousels a year! By 1895, the partners were making so much money that it was rumored the banks were afraid to take their money. So the partners used their newfound wealth to invest in land.

The horses made by the Armitage-Herschell Company were very simple. In fact, they were virtual copies of the animals Allan had seen on that fateful trip to the doctor. They had a folksy look. The ears were upright, carved separately and pinned in for easy replacement in the event they were broken during a move. They had puffy nostrils, a slight smile and an eager look. They had

---

On Herschell's Third Try, "... Throw Same in Canal ..."

Following is an account by Bert Stickney*, who helped Allan Herschell set up and run this third machine:

"It took a cowboy to ride it and it beats all that people were so crazy to ride that we had a devil of a time to keep them from overloading the machine, which had 24 horses and 4 chariots. The machine was of the track type with hinged horses driven by eccentrics. Electric lights were undreamed of, so we lighted the machine with gasoline torches that smoked, filling the canvas top with gasoline fumes. Then too, there was the steam engine and boiler that burned soft coal, generating about as much smoke as it did steam. When the wind blew the smoke toward the machine, some of the people who had paid a perfectly good nickel to ride were a sweet looking sight. Believe me, the public wouldn't stand for that nowadays. Everything's got to be gingerbread, or you don't get their money."

Not only did the machine produce a lot of smoke and noxious fumes, it seems that it broke down a lot. When Allan commented on these problems in a letter to his partners, they responded, "...throw same in canal and return to North Tonawanda, plenty of work in foundry." Allan was so upset by their response that he did not write or otherwise contact them for two months.

* Source is a letter printed in Frederick Fried's *A Pictorial History of the Carousel* (Vestal Press, Ltd., 1964).

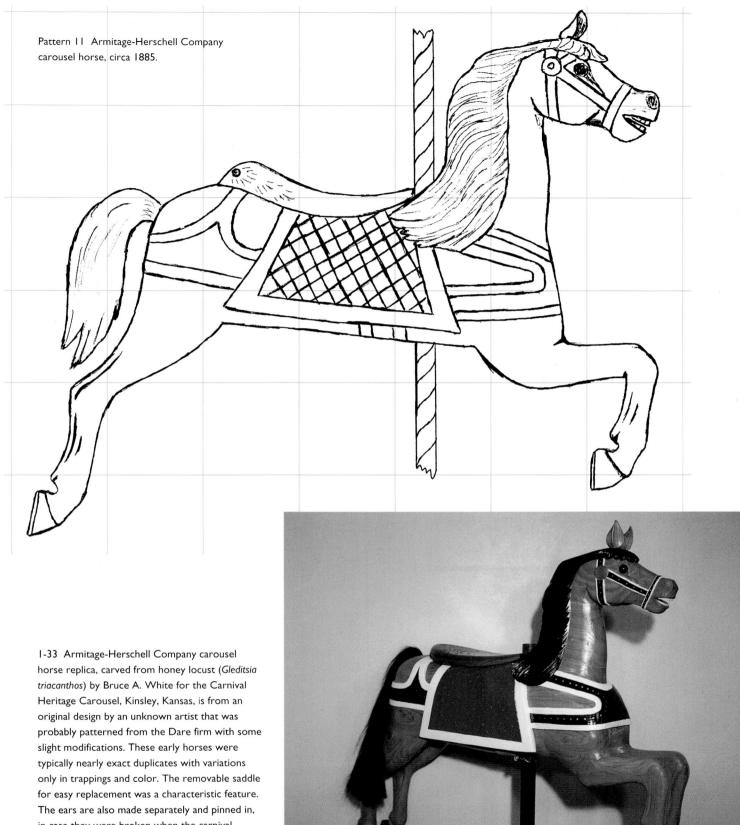

Pattern 11 Armitage-Herschell Company
carousel horse, circa 1885.

1-33 Armitage-Herschell Company carousel
horse replica, carved from honey locust (*Gleditsia
triacanthos*) by Bruce A. White for the Carnival
Heritage Carousel, Kinsley, Kansas, is from an
original design by an unknown artist that was
probably patterned from the Dare firm with some
slight modifications. These early horses were
typically nearly exact duplicates with variations
only in trappings and color. The removable saddle
for easy replacement was a characteristic feature.
The ears are also made separately and pinned in,
in case they were broken when the carnival
moved. Blanket and straps were painted by
Nancy Klenke and Debbie Call. Carving time:
about 50 hours due to the hardness of the wood.

a simple brushed mane rolling to the right with a parted forelock. A simple cavalry saddle, sometimes with an eagle motif etched in the back, was carved separately and nailed or screwed on. They had a fringed, checkered blanket and simple straps. The face was framed in a simple halter. The legs were stiff and stylized and the bodies boxlike. All of the Armitage-Herschell horses were exactly like this with little change until about 1913.

The early horses made by Herschell may have been simple, but they were very charming, and they won hearts the world over. In 1894 alone, his carousels were sold all over the United States and Canada, selling particularly well in the American south. They were also sold in Japan, China, Tahiti, South Africa, Singapore, and India, among other places.

And his carousels made fortunes for some of his customers. The machine he sold in Tahiti is a notable example. The operator didn't have coal available to power it, so he used coconut husks to fuel the boiler. He made so much money from his carousel that he was able to build a resort with a four-story hotel from the profits.

But the bubble burst for the Armitage-Herschell Company in the economic panic of 1899. They had invested heavily in land, which they lost as a result of the panic, and the company was forced into receivership.

When Armitage-Herschell failed, Allan formed a new business with his brother-in-law, Edward Spillman. The new company, formed in 1903, was called the Herschell-Spillman Company. From 1903 to 1920, this company made more carousels than all the other companies operating at that time, combined.

The early horses made by the Herschell-Spillman Company were virtually the same as those that had been made by the Armitage-Herschell Company. But over time, they became more and more refined, eventually rivaling those done by the

Philadelphia and Coney Island firms—especially those done for the larger park machines the company started making in 1913. By 1915, the horses they were producing looked like real horses, not the earlier folksy hobbyhorses. The decor was usually relatively simple. Patriotic themes and flags were common. The figures could be ordered with carved or glass eyes. That some of the figures they made for the park machines were very similar to the Coney Island style is not surprising, since Marcus Illions supplied a set of figures when they started making park machines. The company used duplicate-carving machines extensively so the basic patterns were set by Illions, and the Herschell-Spillman carvers just did the finish carving, adding some touches of their own.

The Herschell-Spillman Company also produced remarkably well-carved menagerie figures — consistently better than even the Philadelphia and Coney Island companies. Their menagerie consisted of lions, tigers, frogs, roosters, dogs, zebras, and pigs.

The carousels made by Herschell-Spillman were not as heavily decorated as those of other companies, but they were also much less expensive. The murals featured a wide variety of mainly pastoral themes. To counter the simplicity of the figures, the chariots were usually richly and ornately carved. Mother Goose, Uncle Sam, and bathing beauties were common themes. Some of the bathing beauties were occasionally a bit risqué.

The Herschell-Spillman Carousel Company added the jumping mechanism to its machines somewhat later than the other companies, not wanting to infringe on existing patents. It became a feature in 1910. Until that time, they made primarily track machines with horses that rocked back and forth. Herschell-Spillman's portable machines were as large as 32 feet; the park machines as large as 50 feet. They even made a few small, hand-cranked machines.

Pattern 12 Herschell-Spillman "Flag Horse" jumper, possibly by C.F. Kopp, circa 1911.

1-34 Herschell-Spillman "Flag Horse" jumper replica was carved from black walnut (*Juglans nigra*) by Bruce A. White as a memorial to Gerald Hermann, an important supporter of the Carnival Heritage Museum, Kinsley, Kansas. The original design is possibly by the "head man," C. F. Kopp, at the Herschell-Spillman firm. Natural wood with flag and straps painted by Cindy White. Carving time: 80 hours.

I-35, I-36, I-37, I-38 (Left, below, and opposite) Herschell-Spillman carousel, Story City, Iowa was made in 1913 in North Tonawanda, New York. P. T. Gifford of Grundy Center, Iowa purchased the carousel from the factory in 1913. It traveled the Iowa countryside for over 20 years, acquired in 1938 from Mr. Gifford by Story City and put into its present location. It was temporarily retired in 1977 to be restored by the Country Shop in Roland, Iowa exactly as it had come from the factory, and reopened in 1982.

A bout of bad health forced Allan into semi-retirement in 1911, but he stayed on as a consultant until 1913, when he went into full retirement. His retirement was short, however, as he came out of retirement in 1915 to start a new company, the Allan Herschell Company, even though the Herschell-Spillman Company was still in operation, now under the full control of the Spillman family.

Allan Herschell may have left the Herschell-Spillman Company to start his own company to undertake the exclusive manufacture of portable machines for traveling carnivals. This had been his initial interest and the original source of his fortune.

When Allan formed his new company in 1915, he used designs from the Herschell-Spillman factory, but he soon developed a new portfolio specifically to address the needs of the traveling carnivals, with their frequent moves, setups and tear downs, loading and unloading. The figures had small compact bodies with short legs drawn up close to the body. The heads were deliberately made oversize with high-set eyes and long, Romanesque noses to grab the attention of prospective riders. They were very aggressive looking. The ears were laid back to minimize the chance of their breaking off when being moved, and the decorations were kept fairly simple.

The carousel horses were painted with painstaking care to counterbalance their simple carving. A lot of pinstriping and filigree was added and the appearance of muscle was achieved through the use of shading. Unfortunately, over the years, the horses' repainting was left to unskilled carnival employees, with predictable results. These garish indifferent paint jobs are what most people today remember from their childhoods, not the meticulously artful factory originals.

While Allan concentrated on making carousels for traveling carnivals, his brother-in-law, Edward, specialized more and more on park machines, still under the name of Herschell-Spillman, even though Allan was no longer with the firm. He finally reorganized in 1920 as the "Spillman Engineering Company."

The horses made by the Spillman Engineering Company had wavy, flowing manes and ornate secondary carving, which distinguished them from the Herschell-Spillman horses. Generally Spillman horses also had shorter necks, longer heads, and heavier, more well-proportioned bodies. Their park machines were not as elaborate as those made by the Philadelphia and Coney Island firms, but they compared quite favorably. The entire carousel was decorated with jewels, beveled mirrors, and relief carvings. The mechanical works were covered with elaborate panels and murals. In addition to the horses, their machines featured a wide variety of very well-carved menagerie animals: lions, tigers, ostriches, storks, cats, dogs, goats, roosters, giraffes, deer, zebras, and frogs. The horses were offered in trotting, galloping, and charging poses. They also made very fine armored horses.

Spillman Engineering did make portable machines, but they were much plainer—usually featuring only horses. The machinery in the center, which ran the carousel, was left open for all to see. The murals and rounding boards were simple affairs.

In the mid-1920s, the Spillman Engineering Company bought a few dozen figures from the by-then defunct Looff carousel factory. The extensive use of duplicate-carving machines and molds explains why many of the later Spillman figures closely resemble Looff's.

By the late 1920s, with more sophisticated carving machines in operation, very little hand carving was being done in either the Allan Herschell Company or Spillman Engineering Company and both were also casting most of the legs and tails from aluminum.

In the 1930s, to cut labor costs and survive the Great Depression, both companies started casting their figures completely from molds, in aluminum. These cast aluminum and later cast fiberglass figures, the molds made from the magnificent creations of the immigrant carvers, are what most people alive today recall. The carvers originally hired by Allan Herschell in the 1880s stayed with him through all the ups and downs and reorganizations, with few exceptions. They showed more and more skill and sophistication in their carving as the years passed. They began with simple hobbyhorses, but in the end created some of the most magnificent carousel figures ever.

Allan Herschell died in 1927 at the age of 76, but his companies continued uninterrupted. The Allan Herschell Company bought out the Spillman Engineering Company in 1945 and continued in business another ten years. In the early 1960s, the molds and assets of the company were bought by

---

◄◎ "Carvers Hall of Fame"

Allan Herschell and Spillman Engineering Company (a partial list*):

Bert Bloomstine

Lloyd Bloomstine

Peter Flack

Fred Jagow

C. F. Kopp — "head man" for Spillman Engineering

Albert Lippich

Richard Lippich

Harry Nightingale

S. P. Paroski

Mr. Rubenburg

Bill Sprenger

* Source, except title, is a Herschell-Spillman list printed in Frederick Fried's *A Pictorial History of the Carousel* (Vestal Press, Ltd., 1964).

Chance Rides, Inc., of Wichita, Kansas. This successor to the Allan Herschell companies continues today as the world's leading manufacturer of carousels, selling their dream weavers worldwide.

The carousels made by Allan Herschell and his associated companies are so common around the world that they are called by a variety of names: Flying Dutchman, Riding Galleries, Flying Horses, and Flying Jennys. But the owners and operators just call them "Tonawanda" machines.

Allan Herschell's companies made more carousels by far than all the other companies combined. This, coupled with the fact that they were made for traveling carnivals and have reached nearly every corner of the globe, is why, when most people think of a merry-go-round, they are thinking of one of Herschell's creations. For this reason, lovers of carousels owe a debt to Allan Herschell.

Charles W. Parker

Charles W. Parker, the self-proclaimed "Colonel Parker, the Amusement King" was born around 1864 in Griggsville, Illinois. He moved by covered wagon with his family to Abilene, Kansas, when he was five years old. His father was a farmer and Charles tried farming when he first struck out on his own. But the long hours, backbreaking labor, and uncertain rewards soon made him give it up. He went through a series of menial jobs, working longest as a janitor at the Dickenson County Courthouse.

Seeking to supplement his income, he ordered a shooting gallery. Before long, he decided he could make a better shooting gallery and started making and selling his own.

Charles saw his first carousel when a traveling carnival came to town, probably about 1890 or '91. He was enchanted by it and persuaded three friends to pitch in with him to buy a small, secondhand one—probably an Armitage-Herschell or, perhaps, a Dare.

Parker and his friends toured the surrounding countryside with this carousel and his shooting gallery. Parker was invigorated by this nomadic life, but his friends weren't. After three years, they gave it up and Parker bought out their shares in the equipment.

As with the shooting gallery, Parker was convinced he could build a better carousel. So he kept tinkering with it and around 1892, he made his first one.

The horses on his early carousels were almost exact duplicates of those made by the Armitage-Herschell Company; in fact, they are sometimes very difficult to tell apart. The main distinguishing features were that the horses made by Parker were not as well put together and were made from poplar (*Populus alba*) rather than the basswood (*Tilia* spp.) and "white" wood (*Pinus strobus*) used by all the other companies. The wood "Colonel" Parker used was technically "poplar," but was a cottonwood. Cottonwood includes several species of the genus *Populus*, but the species (*P. heterophylla*) that grows into giant trees in great profusion in the

ᴥ *Parker Carousel Horses*

Parker horses had long, streamlined bodies with muscles and sinews expressed in interesting ways. The heads were long, thin, and sensitive with the manes rolled back in gentle "S" curves and the forelocks curved back under the ears. Overall, they were stylized but well formed with fancy decorations and lots of glass jewels. The nostrils and ears remained very simple, but the ears were almost always laid back, unlike the perky, upright ears of the earlier horses. The tucked head position was very common. They also did horses with stretched-out heads and necks, and the occasional star gazer. The decorations were a celebration of Americana, with ears of corn, bundles of grapes, and other agricultural products, and guns and other cowboy and Indian accouterments. And, of course, the American flag— every Parker carousel had at least one horse embellished with Old Glory. Flowers also appeared, especially on the few large machines he made for parks. During the Abilene period, his animals reached their highest level of artistry, especially for the large park machines.

Colonel Parker's carvers are not known to have carved any menagerie animals, but they did occasionally appear on his carousels. And they did not resemble anything made in the United States. Judging from their style, especially the placement and attitude of their eyes, I believe the Colonel probably picked them up in his travels from Indonesia.

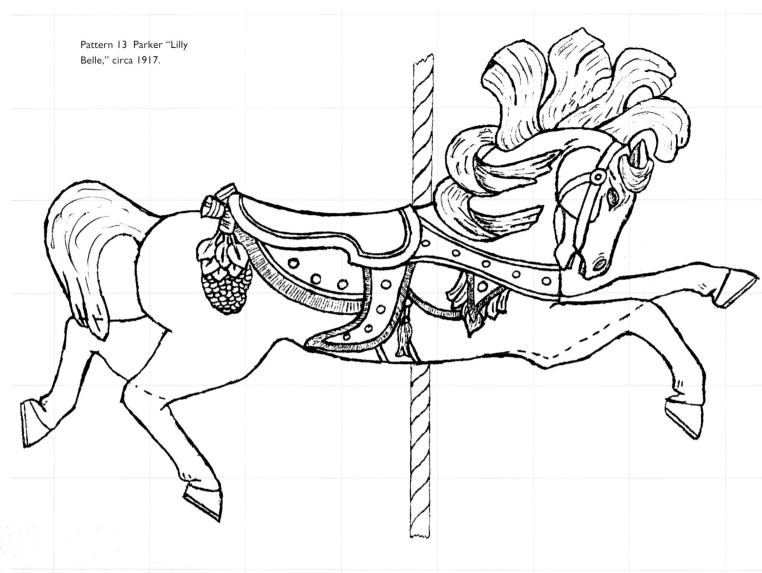

Pattern 13 Parker "Lilly Belle," circa 1917.

1-39 Parker "Lilly Belle" carousel horse replica, carved from cottonwood (*Populus heterophylla*) by Bruce A. White for the Carnival Heritage Carousel, Kinsley, Kansas, is from an original design by an unknown World War I German prisoner of war, held in a camp located in Leavenworth, Kansas. The carving is faithful to the original style, but the head and face are refined and softened. The decorations are similar to those used by the Parker factory prior to World War I, so they were probably originated by Phillip or Eugene Drisco or Loren White. Painted by Charity White Saddler. Carving time: 100 hours.

bottomlands of Kansas is, perhaps, the lowest grade of poplar. Its wood is almost identical in appearance to the poplar (*Populus alba*) in the lumber store. The problem with it is that as it ages, it has a tendency to warp, crack, and twist. It is not a good cabinet grade wood. That wood, coupled with the poor construction techniques his company used, makes Parker Company carousel horses a restoration artist's worst nightmare.

Charles sold his first carousel to his brother Will and used the money to enlarge his factory. He increased his workforce to five people, and named his company the "Parker Carnival Supply Company."

Charles started making not only shooting galleries and carousels, but Ferris wheels and a variety of other carnival rides and devices. He completely outfitted some start-up carnivals. He had outfitted his own complete carnival by 1902. A year later, he had another carnival on the road. By 1906, he had four carnivals on the road. He also created his own publicity mill to stress the cleanliness and high moral character of his carnivals.

Early on, the Colonel hired Joe Applegate, Eugene and Phil Drisco, and Loren White as his carvers. The early efforts of these carvers could charitably be called moderately good folk art. But like the carvers who worked for Allan Herschell, they kept improving. By the turn of the century, they were getting quite good. And they were breaking away from the mold set by the Armitage-Herschell Company and developing their own style. Most were still fairly similar to those made by Armitage-Herschell, but more refined. On the few large park carousels Parker made during this period, his carvers' work compares favorably with that done by the Coney Island firms.

From the designs and master carvings developed by the Drisco brothers and Loren White, duplicate-carving machines roughed out the ponies to be finished by the other carvers.

Although not a carver, Parker closely controlled the output in his factory. He developed a system by which the heads, necks, legs, and tails could be interchanged on various bodies. To facilitate the

1-40 Parker "Lilly Belle" fiberglass casting from a mold made from the original figure, the Parker company's most famous design. It is on a Chance Rides, Inc. carousel at the Bay Pavilion on Pier 57, Seattle, Washington.

1-41, 1-42, 1-43 (Above and opposite) Figures on the Parker carousel, circa 1912, erected each Christmas at the City Center, Seattle, Washington.

swapping of the body parts, the parts were not glued and doweled in place like the other companies', but nailed or screwed into place. This system, of course, has not aided the longevity of his figures.

When you consider the wood the Parker carvers had to work with and the guidelines under which they labored, you have to take your hat off to them.

During the period that Parker had his factory in Abilene, Kansas, it has been rumored, but never proven, that the World War II hero and future president of the United States, Dwight D. Eisenhower, worked for the Colonel sanding carousel horses. This is entirely possible and even likely, as the Parker factory was right across the street from the future president's home until 1911, when it moved to Leavenworth, Kansas. Eisenhower would have been 21 at that time.

Colonel Parker was always anxious to promote his carnivals as wholesome entertainment, especially in Abilene. He encountered particular resistance there from residents who remembered Abilene as a terminus for cattle drives from Texas. The memory of the reputation their town suffered then was stirred by the rowdy "carnies" in their midst, and they didn't welcome them. Bowing to public sentiment, the Colonel moved his entire operation to Leavenworth. Ironically, the city of Abilene now has a museum to celebrate Parker and his achievements not far from the Eisenhower museum.

The Colonel greatly expanded his operation when he relocated to Leavenworth. Nevertheless, he sometimes had to set up his rides in the front yard and on the roof of his factory. In April of 1917, there were 17 carousels, five Ferris wheels, and three monkey speedways set up and being tested. Seven of the carousels were set up on the roof of the factory.

The United States' entry into World War I was a windfall for the Colonel. A German prisoner of war camp was set up in Leavenworth. Parker was able to work out an arrangement whereby some of the German prisoners, gifted artists and craftsmen, were able to help out at his plant. These prisoners introduced some new designs, most notably the "Lilly Belle" or "High Mane" horse so prized by collectors. The horses, while overall retaining the same general appearance as the designs of the Drisco brothers and Loren White, became even more stylized, in fact by far the most stylized carousel horses produced by any company. They retained the same general decorations as those developed by the original Parker Company carvers.

By the end of World War I, bigger and better duplicate-carving machines were being used extensively. The figures became a little stiff in appearance and extremely stylized. As a carousel horse expert, you either like or dislike the late era Parker horses—there isn't much middle ground. They were very aggressive in appearance and very stretched out, with short legs to allow for easy stacking for carnival moves. The decorations, while generally the same as those developed by the original Parker carvers, were rather flat with no protuberances or deep detail. This was partly to decrease the possibility of damage during moves. Another reason for the highly stylized figures with their flat, shallow decor is that this greatly facilitates the use of duplicate-carving machines and molds. This style greatly cuts labor costs, as very little finish carving or cleanup is necessary.

Many of the horses that left the Parker Leavenworth factory were shod with iron horseshoes. Imprinted on them was "11 Worth" to represent "Leavenworth."

Parker died in 1932 in his Leavenworth mansion at the age of 68. His son carried on

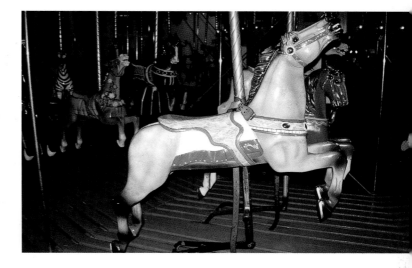

for several more years before closing the doors. In the 1950s, a company called Theel Manufacturing, located in Leavenworth, bought the assets from the company, including the molds the Parker Company used toward the end. They continued to manufacture Parker style carousels, casting the carousel figures from aluminum, until the late 1980s.

In October 2000, the city manager of Leavenworth, hearing that my factory had burned down in Kinsley, Kansas, graciously extended an invitation to me to move my operation there and perpetuate the town's carousel legacy. I declined the invitation, preferring to rebuild in St. Joseph, Missouri, where my carousel is located at the Patee House/Pomy Express/Jesse James Museum.

CHAPTER 2

Dream Weavers: Original Carousel Creations

My passion for carving was first awakened while I was on a naval tour of duty in the Mediterranean, where I discovered the works of Michelangelo and the other Renaissance masters. From the first, I was enraptured, standing before the works of these masters for hours, studying them to the most minute detail. I had never taken an art course, but to do so was suddenly an intense desire. Later, back in the States, I was walking through an art show with my daughter Amirina on my shoulders when I noticed an old man carving a beautiful owl. I must have watched him for an hour. Finally, I said to him, "I sure wish I could do that." That old man looked me right in the eye and said, "The proof of desire is pursuit." He went back to work, not knowing how deeply he had impressed me.

Several years later I had the opportunity to apprentice to a man who carved plaques for servicemen when they were transferred or discharged. When he left I carved a plaque for him and he said, " Bruce, you are the master now." I was transferred to Japan, where I carved an extremely intricate Chinese dragon in the round, just for myself. My wife was very proud of it and entered the piece in an art competition at a local Japanese department store. The piece won Best of Show and made headlines in the local papers. My Japanese friends started calling me "Tensai" White, a word

2-1 (FACING PAGE) Katie Payne of Fort Leavenworth, Kansas takes a spin on the original full-size carving of "Ms. Applebee," on the "Wild Thing" carousel in operation as part of the Patee House/ Pony Express/Jesse James Museum in St. Joseph, Missouri. Copies can be found in over 1,000 Applebee restaurants worldwide. The head resembles a horse done by Daniel Muller, but the style is otherwise very much Bruce's. Carved in basswood (*Tilia* spp.), painted by Nancy Klenke. Carving time: 120 hours.

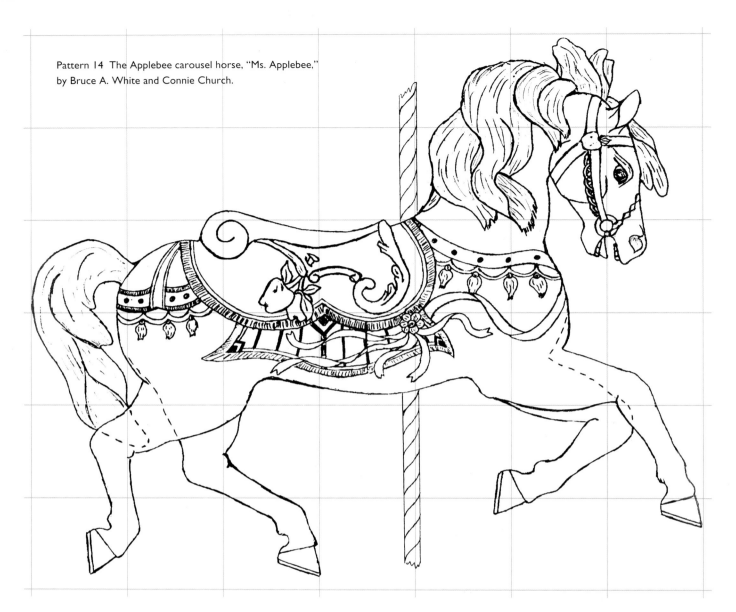

Pattern 14 The Applebee carousel horse, "Ms. Applebee," by Bruce A. White and Connie Church.

closely related to *sensei* or teacher, but the superlative form, a very great honor. After my release from the Navy, I entered the art show circuit, participating in juried fine art shows and exhibits. I focused primarily on wildlife sculpture.

I made my first carousel horse when I was 34, only because it was a commissioned request. But a carousel rocking horse I was carving at the time appeared in a local newspaper article and caught the attention of a toy manufacturer; he produced a popular spring-ride hobbyhorse and was looking for a new model maker. This led to my making prototype models for Wonder Toys. After several years I was determined to strike out on my own.

Years of planning, hard work, and hardship followed, as well as the reward of some satisfying accomplishments. My work is exhibited worldwide in Applebee restaurants; my Endangered Species series of carousel animals were a huge success for Chance Rides, Inc., and have been placed on carousels all over the world; using the Endangered Species figures, I created my own carousel, the "Wild Thing," which thrills thousands of children every month, and in the creation of which I produced the molds and gained the expertise to manufacture carousels for sale. I've known devastating loss too: fire, the scourge of the carousel world, was visited on me in the summer of 2000.

The Applebee Carousel Horse

Copies of this carousel horse can be found in Applebee's restaurants all over the United States, Canada, Mexico, Central America, Europe, and the Middle East. In fact, they can be found on every continent except Antarctica. In one month, I sent four to Athens: two to Athens, Greece, one to Athens, Georgia, and one to Athens, Texas.

This carousel horse is probably the work that most people associate with me because it is on public display in Applebee's restaurants worldwide. Unfortunately, like the other figures I have done for molding and reproduction, it is not my best work. The mold-making and casting process imposes limitations; there can be no sharp edges or deep undercuts. However, because of the refined manufacturing process I have developed over the past five years, the result is far more detailed than anything my competitors can produce.

The Applebee carousel horse is a successful example of the exercise of long-term planning and bulldog determination. I like to paraphrase the adage about necessity as "poverty is the mother of invention." If I can't do it the way the companies with lots of capital do it, I just find another way.

⚭ The Original Applebee Carousel Horse

In April of 1995, I presented Connie Church and Rocky Brock of Applebee's with the number one copy of the Applebee carousel horse. It was installed—after being painted seven times to get the color scheme just right—at the Applebee's Restaurant in Shawnee Mission, Kansas, where it still stands today. The original carving is on my carousel at the Pony Express Historical Society in St. Joseph, Missouri. This horse is used to demonstrate painting in the section "Finishing & Painting Techniques," pages 133 to 139, at the end of Chapter 5.

In the mid 1990s the Applebee restaurant chain had about 500 restaurants in the United States. A major decorative element in all of them was the carousel horse I had carved for the spring-ride hobbyhorse manufacturer Wonder Toys, which had launched my carousel-carving career (refer to 1-14). But I did not own the rights to this design. So I persistently approached Applebee's over a long period to pitch a better carousel horse to be designed exclusively for them. Their headquarters

2-2 Miniature versions of the "Ms. Applebee" carousel figure are carved from lacewood (*Cardwellia sublimis*). Carving time: 40 hours.

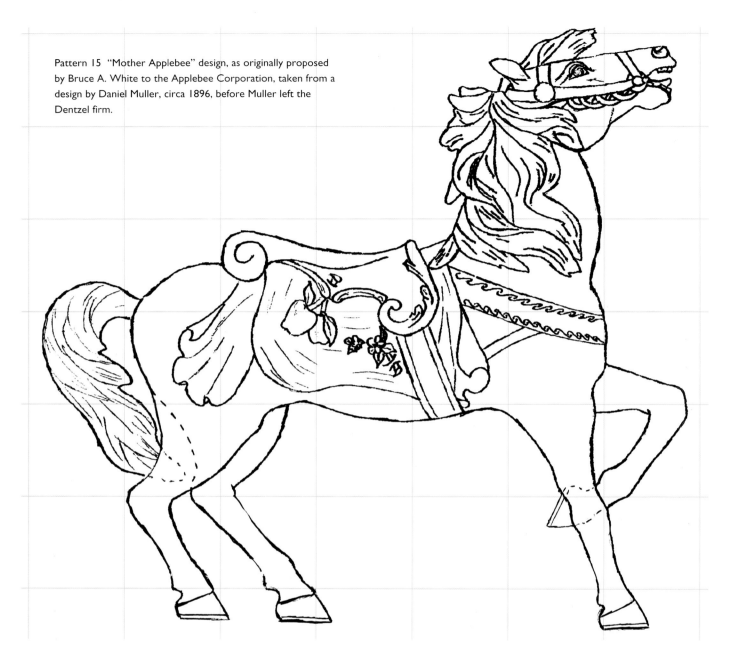

Pattern 15 "Mother Applebee" design, as originally proposed by Bruce A. White to the Applebee Corporation, taken from a design by Daniel Muller, circa 1896, before Muller left the Dentzel firm.

was nearby and they were about to open restaurants in Europe, but it was no easy task getting them to consider my ideas.

Finally, I caught the ear of Connie Church, who was responsible for interior design. She was intrigued, and it was decided that we would work together on a design for an Applebee trademark carousel horse. I would carve the prototype on my own time and at my own expense. A decision as to whether or not the Applebee Corporation would use it would be made based on their critique of my original carving. The instant Connie Church and

Rocky Brock, the head of equipment purchasing, saw the prototype carving they were sold. But I still had to prove that I could manufacture them.

I was casting the figures from fiberglass at that time. This had been the prevailing technique for over 30 years, but it produced one figure in about two days. It required another two to three days to assemble the parts and do the finish work, and two days more to paint it. So I could comfortably put out three or four horses a month by myself in my home shop. I needed no employees, and my overhead was very low.

But the increased volume with the Applebee contract quickly became more than I could handle and I had to find a way to increase efficiency and production capacity. Most frustrating to me was that my time was completely tied up with the manufacture of Applebee horses and I had no time for new carving, which is where my heart lies. I had worked very hard to get this contract to subsidize my work as an artist, and now I had no time to be an artist.

About this time I made the acquaintance of a very remarkable woman, Nancy Klenke. She was a hard worker and a fine painter, exactly what I needed. She very quickly became indispensable. But even with Nancy's help, the workload was overwhelming. I had to find a better way.

An experiment with polyurethane foam cut my production time in half, to two days, faster than anyone else's, except the manufacturer of the horse based on my design that Applebee's had been using earlier. They used a spin casting machine, which was prohibitively expensive. I hired an experienced high-density foam sprayer, Jack Ayers, to fill the molds.

At a carnival that came to town, my daughter Charity asked to go on an amusement ride called a "Space Ball." The operator strapped the rider into a seat and turned the contraption by hand to tumble the rider in all different directions. What I saw was essentially a spin casting machine, only smaller and vastly cheaper. The next day, I discussed the idea with Jack, who thought his son could make a similar machine for me.

Only a month later, I had my first prototype spin caster, and I cut my production time to six hours. Eventually, a larger, sturdier spin caster was designed and it started to render my dream a reality. I was now able to fulfill the Applebee contract for which I had worked so hard. Remaining problems in the finishing were solved over the next three years.

✏ *Carousels with Figures by Bruce A. White*

Carousels with original figures made by the author include:

The "Wild Thing" carousel, 21 figures and one bench, Patee House/ Pony Express/Jesse James Museum, St. Joseph, MO.

Kansas Children Designed Carousel, including 5 figures designed by Kansas school children, Carnival Heritage Center, Kinsley, KS.

Carnival Heritage Carousel, 32 reproduction carvings of designs originated by masters of the Golden Age of the Carousel (circa 1879–1929), on a circa 1900 double-decker carousel, completion date of Fall 2003, Carnival Heritage Center, Kinsley, KS,

Carousels that include reproductions of figures carved by the author:

CAROUSELS MADE BY CAROUSELS USA OF SAN ANTONIO, TX:

Wildlife World Zoo, Litchfield Park, AZ.

Encino Place Mall, Beverly Hills, CA.

Lion Country Safari, Loxahatchee, FL.

Miller Park Zoo, Bloomington, IL.

Hickory Crawdads Baseball, Hickory, NC.

Winston-Salem Warthogs Baseball, Winston-Salem, NC.

Charlotte Knights Baseball, Fort Mill, SC.

CAROUSELS MADE BY CHANCE RIDES, INC., WICHITA, KS (partial list):

Marineland, San Diego, CA.

Guadalupe Park Arena Green, San Jose, CA.

Animal Park, Inc., Gulf Breeze, FL.

Lowry Park, Tampa, FL.

Niabi Zoo, Cole Valley, IL.

Omaha Zoo, Omaha, NE.

Dallas Zoo, Dallas, TX.

Carousel horses made by the author when he worked for Roto Cast/ Wonder Toys are also included on carousels made by Bertalzon Carousels of Milan, Italy and Luna Park Carousels of Buenos Aires, Argentina.

The Applebee carousel horses made by the author can be found in over 1,000 Applebee restaurants across the United States, Canada, and Mexico as well as in Guatemala, Honduras. Nicaragua, Sweden, The Netherlands, Spain, Germany, Greece, Egypt, and Kuwait.

Original carvings by the author are found in private collections in the United States, Japan, England, and Kuwait.

Endangered Species

A successful artist learns early that if he or she doesn't want to remain a starving artist, he must do two things: first and most important, he must have a means of support other than his art. The second is always to keep lots of irons in the fire.

The first problem I tackled with my training as a paramedic—I had often fallen back on it to make ends meet—and with the steady employment of my wife Cindy. Without her support, both emotionally and financially, I could never have pursued my dream as an artist.

In the second area, I have emulated C. W. Parker. I employ a two-person publicity mill: my wife and myself. My dozens of newspaper and magazine articles and television and radio interviews didn't just happen. Cindy and I worked hard to make them happen. We spent a lot of time telling people how great I am, even if I'm not really the greatest sculptor. If you persist long enough, a funny thing happens: people actually start to believe you. After all, they read it in the paper, right?

This is how Chance Rides, Inc., of Wichita, Kansas—the successor to the Allan Herschell companies—came to know of me. They wanted one

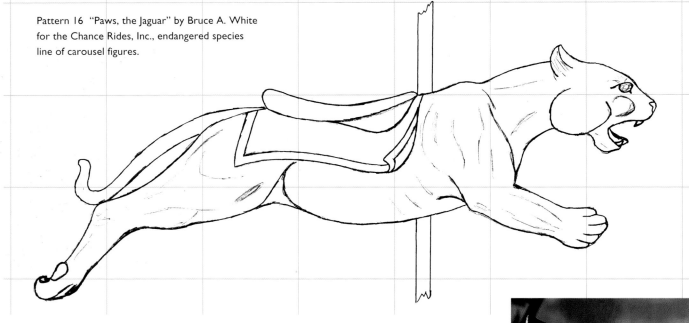

Pattern 16 "Paws, the Jaguar" by Bruce A. White for the Chance Rides, Inc., endangered species line of carousel figures.

2-3, 2-4 "Paws, the Jaguar," No. 1 copy of the original design and carving by Bruce A. White for the Chance Rides, Inc., endangered species line of carousel figures. The original carving in basswood (*Tilia* spp.) was carved as a generic panther so it could be painted to resemble a leopard, jaguar, or cougar, but it most closely resembles a jaguar in body conformation and the size and shape of the head; it was donated by Chance to the Sedgwick County Zoo in Wichita, Kansas. Painted by Charity White Saddler. Carving time of original: 60 hours.

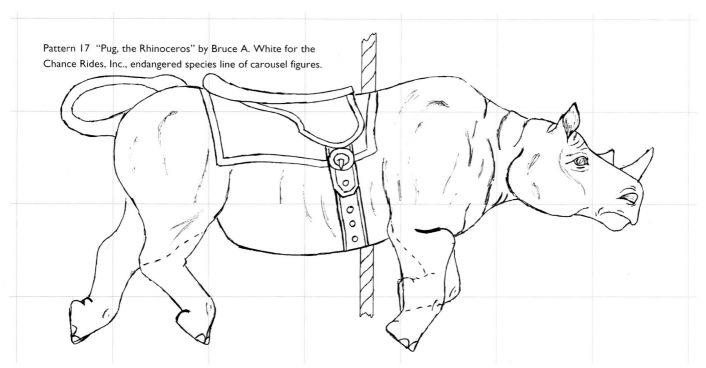

Pattern 17 "Pug, the Rhinoceros" by Bruce A. White for the Chance Rides, Inc., endangered species line of carousel figures.

of the best carvers around to create a new line of animals for their carousels; reading several articles about me persuaded them that I was the man. They first contacted me while I was pestering Applebee's, and explained that they intended to expand their line of carousel animals to include a number of endangered species. Would I carve the original wood models for them? Following my practice of keeping several irons in the fire, I agreed.

It was over a year later that they called me back; I was then caught up in trying to find a way to meet my commitment to Applebee's and had long since given up on Chance as a source of work. Now they were ready to start work on the endangered species carousel figures. Could I provide them four over the course of the next year, they asked. I guess I've always had more optimism than brains, so I said yes, even though at the time I had no idea how I could satisfy even the Applebee commitment.

By the time I did find a way to fulfill my contract with Applebee's, I had only three months remaining to carve those four figures for Chance. I had not done even the background research for the figures: a panther, a rhinoceros, an elephant, and a gorilla.

2-5 "Pug, the Rhinoceros," No. 1 copy of the original design and carving by Bruce A. White for the Chance Rides, Inc., endangered species line of carousel figures. The original carving in basswood (*Tilia* spp.) was donated by Chance to the Sedgwick County Zoo in Wichita, Kansas, where the model, a black rhino, resides. Painted by Arinda Jones. Carving time of original: 80 hours.

2-6 The miniature carving from Honduran mahogany (*Swietenia macrophylla*) of "Pug, the Rhinoceros." Carving time: 15 hours.

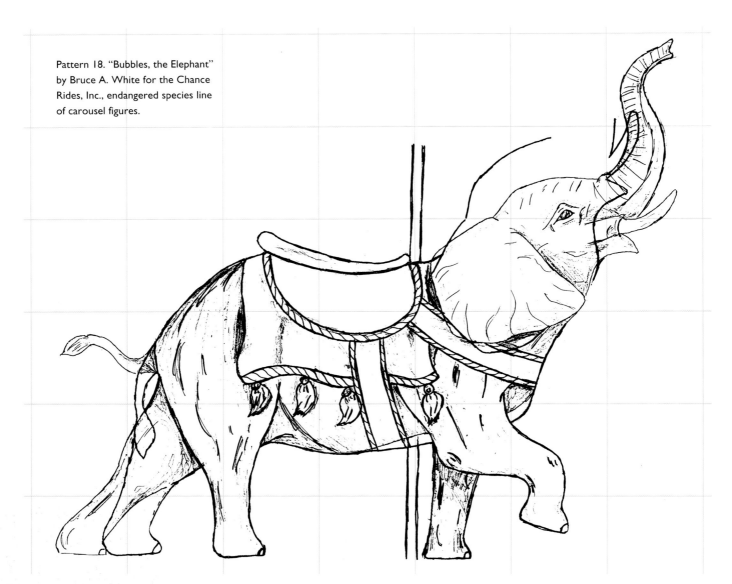

Pattern 18. "Bubbles, the Elephant" by Bruce A. White for the Chance Rides, Inc., endangered species line of carousel figures.

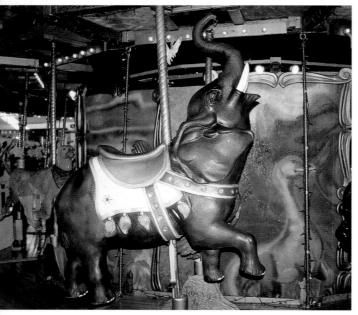

2-7 (Left) "Bubbles, the Elephant," No. 1 copy of the original design and carving by Bruce A. White for the Chance Rides, Inc., endangered species line of carousel figures. The original carving in basswood (*Tilia* spp.) was donated by Chance to the Sedgwick County Zoo in Wichita, Kansas, where the model, an African elephant, resides. Painted by Cindy White. Carving time of original: 90 hours.

2-8 (Right) The miniature carving from basswood (*Tilia* spp.) of "Bubbles, the Elephant." Carving time: 20 hours.

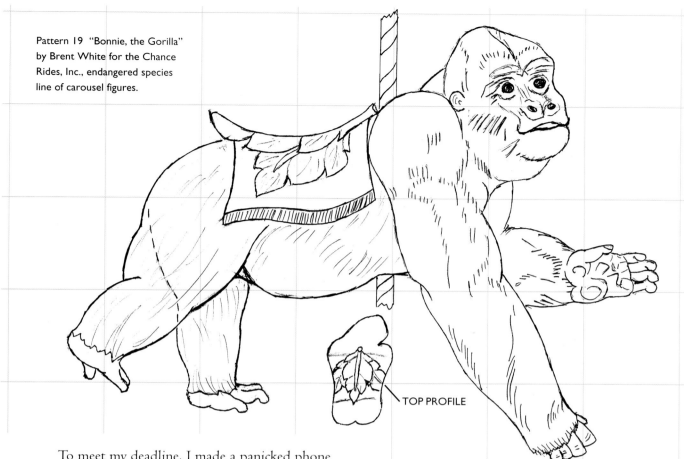

Pattern 19 "Bonnie, the Gorilla" by Brent White for the Chance Rides, Inc., endangered species line of carousel figures.

TOP PROFILE

To meet my deadline, I made a panicked phone call to my brother Brent, who helped me carve the gorilla. He did the research, design, initial cut-out, glue-up, and rough shaping for the gorilla, and I did the detail carving and finish work. I finished the figures just days before deadline. They now inhabit Chance carousels all over the world.

2-9 The miniature of "Bonnie, the Gorilla" carved from Honduran mahogany (*Swietenia macrophylla*) by Brent White. Carving time: 15 hours.

2-10 "Bonnie, the Gorilla," No. 2 copy of the original, designed and rough shaped by Brent White with detail carving and finish work by Bruce A. White for the Chance Rides, Inc., endangered species line of carousel figures. The original carving in basswood (*Tilia* spp.) was donated by Chance to the Sedgwick County Zoo in Wichita, Kansas. The model was Pete, the gorilla, of the Seattle Zoo, where the No. 1 copy was donated. Painted by Arinda Jones. Carving time of original: 80 hours.

2-11 Bruce A. White's carousel, "Wild Thing," once a fixture at a local shopping center, is continuing to delight children and adults as part of the Patee House/Pony Express/Jesse James Museum in St. Joseph, Missouri.

2-12 Van Hopkins of St. Joseph, Missouri, age 2½, a regular, always rides "Rose" on the "Wild Thing" carousel.

Wild Things & Other Designs

The "Wild Thing" Carousel

Flush with success and my company on a firm footing at last in 1998, I became obsessed with creating my own carousel. This was something I had wanted to do since carving my first carousel figure in 1989, but it had always been beyond my grasp. After all, how does a poor boy from Kansas make a carousel worth hundreds of thousands of dollars in this modern age? The answer is, through long-range planning and long, backbreaking hours of work.

I had learned from past mistakes, so I did not give Chance Rides, Inc, exclusive rights to the endangered species figures I made for them—I maintained the copyrights. As I carved each of the figures, I had made a mold of it. I had been carving figures from the time I first conceived the idea of making a carousel nearly ten years earlier. Now I actually had enough figures to populate one. But I had no frame to put them on and certainly not enough money to buy a new one, or even a used one that still worked. I managed to locate an old, inoperable 1941 Allan Herschell carousel frame and persuaded my bank to finance the purchase.

After nearly a year of work, done primarily in the evenings and on weekends, the "Wild Thing" carousel was a long-awaited dream come true. It was truly a family affair: my brother Brent carved new shields to replace the original Indian heads and the Dreamer's Bench; my son Zachary did most

2-13 (Left) Every carousel must have a bench, and the "Dreamer's Bench" carved from maple (*Acer* spp.) by Brent White for Bruce's "Wild Thing" carousel was excitement enough for Desiree Dilliehurt of St. Joseph, Missouri with her brother John. Painted by Brent's daughter, Brianna, and Bruce's wife, Cindy.

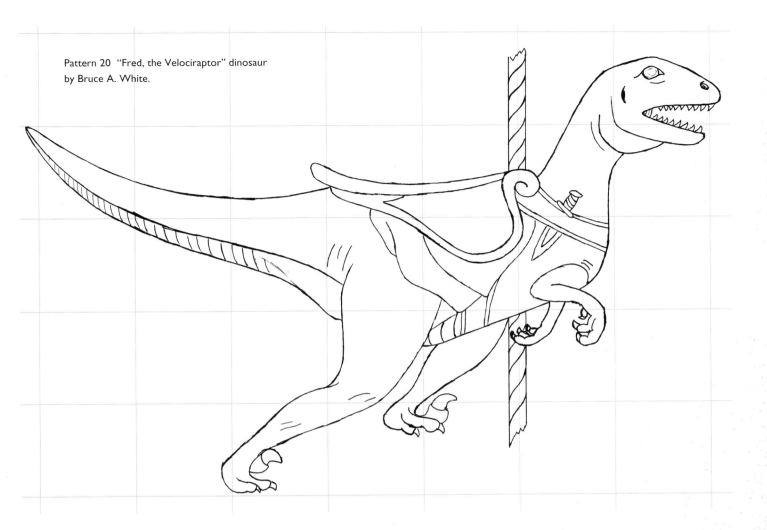

Pattern 20 "Fred, the Velociraptor" dinosaur
by Bruce A. White.

❧ An Education in Carousel Construction

The 1941 Allan Herschell carousel frame I bought was a total wreck—actually not worth a nickel, let alone the money I paid for it—but it gave me a blueprint from which to work. I had wanted to retain as much of the original frame as possible, but soon discovered there was very little that was salvageable. In the end, the only original remaining parts on my carousel frame were the tower, the sweeps, the ring gear, and the rocker arms.

While I was rebuilding the frame and finishing the animals for it, my daughter Charity painted all new center murals and murals for the rounding boards from sketches prepared by my good friend Pete Fedder.

2-14 "Fred, the Velociraptor" dinosaur carved from poplar (*Populus alba*) by Bruce A. White is on his "Wild Thing" carousel at the Patee House/ Pony Express/Jesse James Museum in St. Joseph, Missouri. Copies of this original are found on carousels across the United States made by Carousels USA of San Antonio, Texas. Painted by Charity White Saddler. Carving time: 40 hours.

of the rewiring and helped me with other heavy "grunt labor"; my daughter Charity painted all the murals; my daughter Jacquie drew up the business plan to operate the carousel profitably and acted as its manager for the first six months. My daughters Gladys and Amirina gave invaluable moral support and spent hours as my "sounding boards," as did my parents, Jack and Melva White, who also gave me financial support. Last, but certainly not least, my most ardent supporter, my wife Cindy, helped in every facet of the "Wild Thing," from the first day I conceived of it.

The "Wild Thing" carousel included the Endangered Species figures and the figures created for the San Jose Carousel, as described below, as well as many other designs. It opened October 2, 1999, at the East Hills Mall in St. Joseph, Missouri, and brought joy to tens of thousands of children. I am truly blessed as one of the few people who has actually seen how their work can bring happiness to others. It has been such a thrill to watch the children and hear their laughter as I worked on my latest carousel creation. The poem Pete wrote for me, which is at the front of this book, is a true story.

I have since donated the "Wild Thing" carousel to the Pony Express Historical Society in St. Joseph. It now has a permanent home at the Patee House/Pony Express/Jesse James Museum. A beautiful brick building has been built to house it, and the "Wild Thing" carousel works its magic on the young and young-at-heart again.

The San Jose Carousel

I finished the Endangered Species figures for Chance Rides, Inc., just days before the major trade show for the carnival and amusement industries, where Chance writes most of their orders for the coming year. The Endangered Species figures were a big hit. One of the orders they wrote was for the city of San Jose, California. But there was one catch; they wanted some special figures in addition to the Endangered Species animals and would place the order only if the carver of the original figures also carved these special ones.

The city of San Jose was in the midst of a revitalization project. As part of the project, the professional hockey team, the San Jose Sharks, had

2-15 The copy of "Sam, the Eagle" on Bruce's "Wild Thing" carousel was modified to have an accessible bench seat, inspired by thoughts of his painter, Nancy Klenke, who after painting more than 500 carousel animals, was limited by a disability to riding only on the standard bench seat of a carousel. The figure is popular not only with people who have a disability, but also with parents or grandparents holding a baby, as well as with friends and sweethearts of all ages, since it seats two.

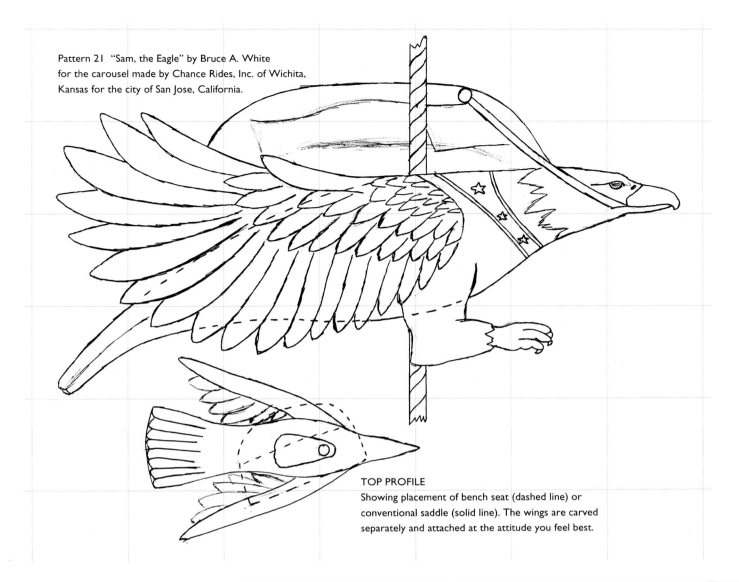

Pattern 21 "Sam, the Eagle" by Bruce A. White for the carousel made by Chance Rides, Inc. of Wichita, Kansas for the city of San Jose, California.

TOP PROFILE
Showing placement of bench seat (dashed line) or conventional saddle (solid line). The wings are carved separately and attached at the attitude you feel best.

2-16 The original carving from basswood (*Tilia* spp.) of "Sam, the Eagle" in Bruce's shop has a typical saddle on its back, on which the rider sits astride as on any other carousel animal. Carving time: 200 hours.

Pattern 22 "Ruby, the Hummingbird" by Bruce A. White for the carousel made by Chance Rides, Inc. of Wichita, Kansas for the city of San Jose, California.

TOP PROFILE

2-17 This is the No. 1 copy of the "Ruby, the Hummingbird" figure done for the San Jose city carousel. It is patterned after a ruby-throated hummingbird. Painted by Nancy Klenke. Carved from basswood (*Tilia* spp.), this figure with all of the feathers and birds, took longer to carve than any other carousel figure Bruce has done: 280 hours.

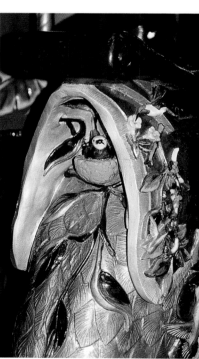

2-18 (Right) The hummingbird just under the saddle is a life-sized ruby-throated hummingbird. The two hummingbirds hovering just below over the trumpet creeper vine are life-sized Cuban Bee hummingbirds. The one hovering over the hibiscus is a life-sized giant Peruvian hummingbird, and nestled in its nest under the saddle is a Rufous hummingbird.

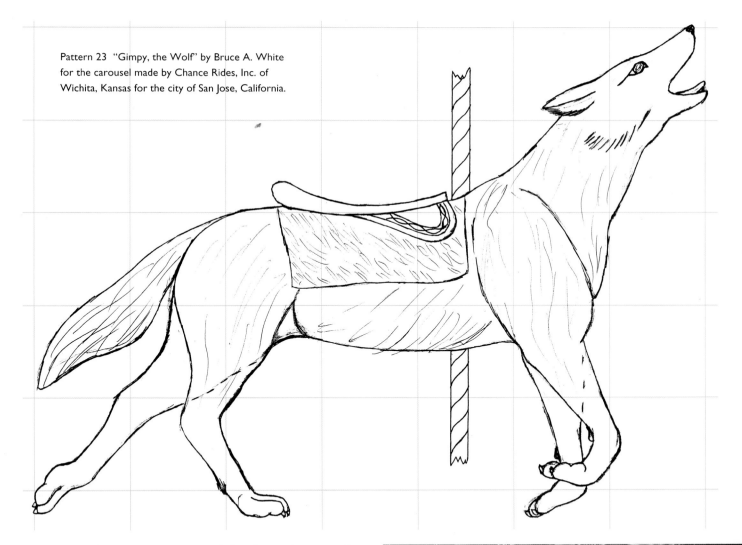

Pattern 23 "Gimpy, the Wolf" by Bruce A. White for the carousel made by Chance Rides, Inc. of Wichita, Kansas for the city of San Jose, California.

agreed to finance a carousel for the park across the street from their stadium. The city of San Jose is built on land that originally belonged to the Aloni Indians. Four animals are sacred in their religion: the eagle, the hummingbird, the coyote, and the salmon. To pay respect to the Aloni Indians, the city officials of San Jose wanted these figures on their carousel. Since the San Jose Sharks were paying for the project, they wanted a shark for the carousel, too.

Designs for the coyote, hummingbird, salmon, and shark were pretty easy for me to come up with. But the eagle was a challenge. The city officials wanted the wings to be spread for dramatic effect, but it couldn't take up more than one allotted space on the carousel. I came up with a design in which the wings were thrown back as if the eagle were in a dive . . . not completely realistic or natural, but close.

2-19 This is the No. 1 copy in basswood (*Tilia* spp.) of the "Gimpy, the Wolf" figure done for the San Jose city carousel. Bruce's use of wolf photographs from *National Geographic* magazine resulted in coverage of his work on the piece appearing in the September 1998 issue of *National Geographic*. Painted by Charity White Saddler. Carving time: 60 hours.

Pattern 24 "Patty, the Salmon" by Mike Meister, formerly of Chance, and Brent White for the carousel made by Chance Rides, Inc. of Wichita, Kansas for the city of San Jose, California.

2-20 Chris Kramer of Maryville, Missouri rides the ocean waves on "Patty, the Salmon" on the "Wild Thing" carousel while his mother, Ella, keeps him on. This is the No. 1 copy in basswood (*Tilia* spp.) of the figure done for the San Jose city carousel. As with many of the figures for the San Jose carousel, the salmon was chosen by the city because it is a sacred animal to the Aloni Indians, the people indigenous to the area. The figure was cut-out, glued-up, and rough shaped by Brent White with detail carving and finishing by Bruce. Painted by Charity White Saddler. Carving time: 50 hours.

It was initially rejected as being too hard for a rider to get on and dismount. Eventually it was accepted, as there seemed to be no reasonable alternative.

Applebee's production was running more or less smoothly by then, but money problems caused delays. As with the Endangered Species figures, I finished only days before deadline, again with the help of my brother Brent. He did the cut-out, glue-up, and rough shaping for the salmon, and I did the detail carving and finishing.

I was invited to the grand opening of the San Jose carousel, which was held December 15, 1998, and was given special recognition at the dedication ceremony. It was one of the proudest moments of my life, especially since the months while carving these figures before the opening of the carousel were some of the most difficult. I could not have gotten through them without the help of my assistants and the support of my family.

Pattern 25 "Mako, the Shark" by Bruce A. White, modeled after the logo for the professional hockey team, the San Jose Sharks, who financed the carousel made by Chance Rides, Inc. of Wichita, Kansas for the city of San Jose, California.

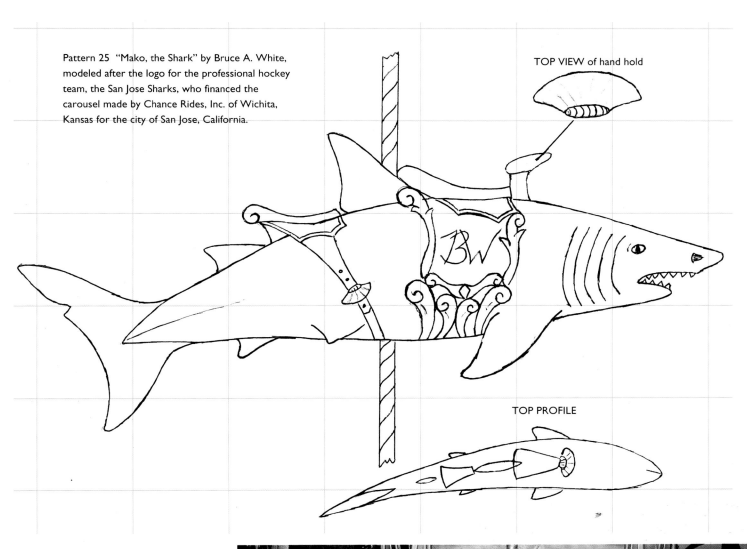

TOP VIEW of hand hold

TOP PROFILE

2-21 After making "Mako, the Shark" for the San Jose city carousel, using the hockey team logo as the model, Bruce carved a two-seater shark from basswood (*Tilia* spp.) for his "Wild Thing" carousel that he wanted to be realistic, but not frighten small children. Painted by Charity White Saddler. Carving time: 50 hours.

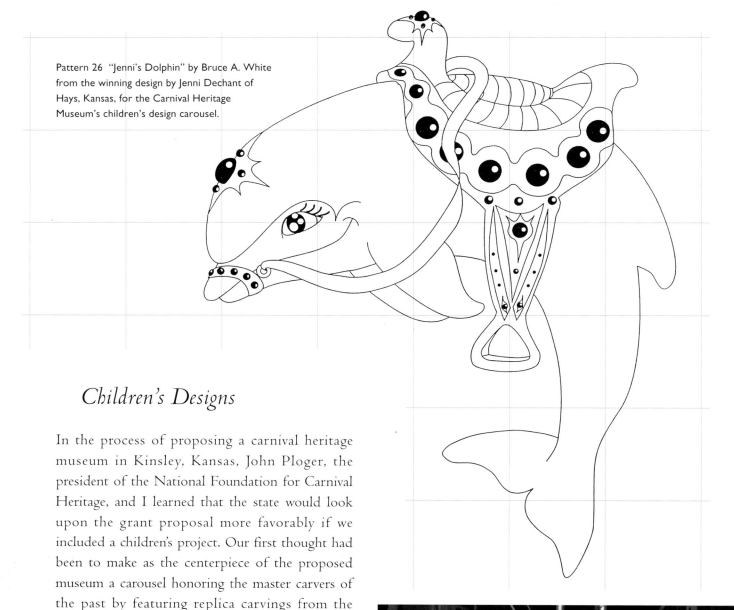

Pattern 26 "Jenni's Dolphin" by Bruce A. White from the winning design by Jenni Dechant of Hays, Kansas, for the Carnival Heritage Museum's children's design carousel.

Children's Designs

In the process of proposing a carnival heritage museum in Kinsley, Kansas, John Ploger, the president of the National Foundation for Carnival Heritage, and I learned that the state would look upon the grant proposal more favorably if we included a children's project. Our first thought had been to make as the centerpiece of the proposed museum a carousel honoring the master carvers of the past by featuring replica carvings from the companies that had supplied the Kinsley carnivals.

But with the state's bias in mind, John and I devised a "Design a Carousel Animal Contest" for Kansas schoolchildren. We rewrote the proposal to have as the museum's eventual centerpiece a carousel designed completely by those who love them the most, children.

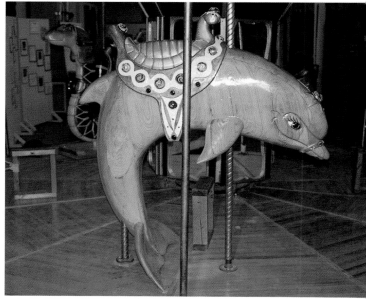

2-22 "Jenni's Dolphin" carved from red oak (*Quercus rubra*) by Bruce A. White, and left with a clear wood finish to show the beauty of the wood. Oak was chosen for this figure because the bold grain pattern is reminiscent of an ocean's waves. The glass baubles were blown by John Winter of Kinsley, Kansas. Saddle painted by Nancy Klenke. Carving time: 70 hours.

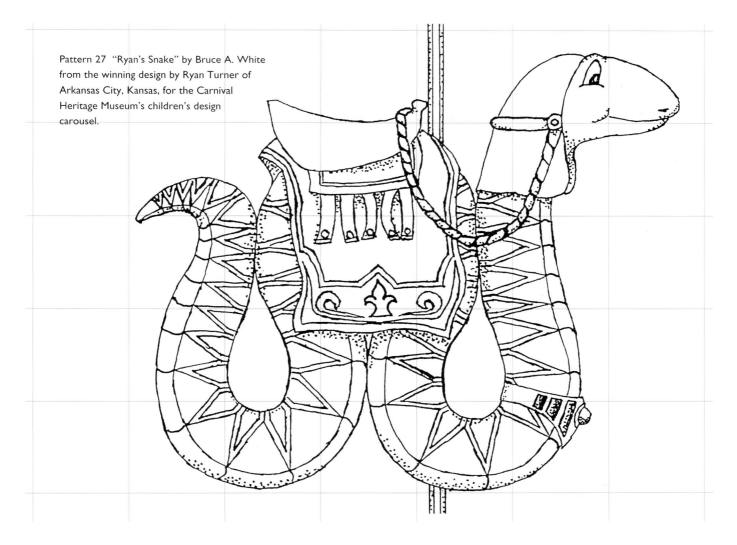

Pattern 27 "Ryan's Snake" by Bruce A. White from the winning design by Ryan Turner of Arkansas City, Kansas, for the Carnival Heritage Museum's children's design carousel.

The National Foundation for Carnival Heritage was awarded a grant from the state to renovate a building for the museum, and another grant through the National Endowment for the Arts to help fund the centerpiece carousel to be designed by children.

A great deal of hard work made the museum a reality, and it opened its doors in May of 1996. The unveiling of the first year's winning design was part of the opening ceremony. The children's carousel design contest has generated a great deal of interest in Kansas, and each year thousands of entries are received from all over the state. To date, I have completed figures for an Egyptian Snake designed by Ryan Turner of Arkansas City, Kansas, 1996; a Roadrunner designed by Joseph Astrabe of Winfield, Kansas, 1997; a Dolphin designed by

2-23 "Ryan's Snake," carved from pine (*Pinus strobus*) by Bruce A. White. Painted by Charity White Saddler. Carving time: 80 hours.

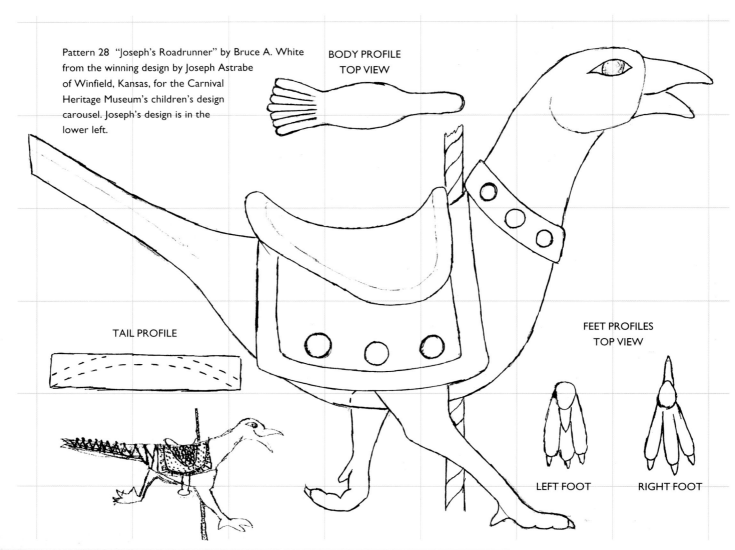

Pattern 28 "Joseph's Roadrunner" by Bruce A. White from the winning design by Joseph Astrabe of Winfield, Kansas, for the Carnival Heritage Museum's children's design carousel. Joseph's design is in the lower left.

BODY PROFILE
TOP VIEW

TAIL PROFILE

FEET PROFILES
TOP VIEW

LEFT FOOT

RIGHT FOOT

2-24 "Joseph's Roadrunner," carved from Honduran mahogany (*Swietenia macrophylla*) by Bruce A. White, and left with a clear wood finish to show the beauty of the wood. Mahogany was chosen for this figure because the color of the wood is reminiscent of the sandstone mesas of the United States southwest desert, where roadrunners make their home. The glass baubles were blown by John Winter of Kinsley, Kansas. Blanket and saddle painted by Charity White Saddler. Carving time: 40 hours.

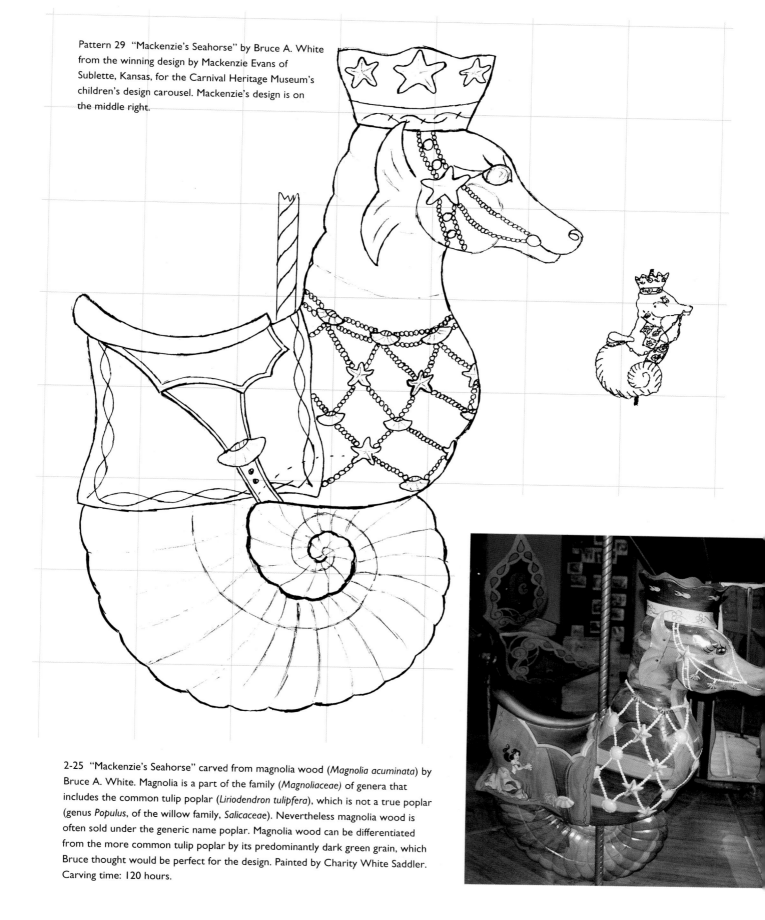

Pattern 29 "Mackenzie's Seahorse" by Bruce A. White from the winning design by Mackenzie Evans of Sublette, Kansas, for the Carnival Heritage Museum's children's design carousel. Mackenzie's design is on the middle right.

2-25 "Mackenzie's Seahorse" carved from magnolia wood (*Magnolia acuminata*) by Bruce A. White. Magnolia is a part of the family (*Magnoliaceae*) of genera that includes the common tulip poplar (*Liriodendron tulipfera*), which is not a true poplar (genus *Populus*, of the willow family, *Salicaceae*). Nevertheless magnolia wood is often sold under the generic name poplar. Magnolia wood can be differentiated from the more common tulip poplar by its predominantly dark green grain, which Bruce thought would be perfect for the design. Painted by Charity White Saddler. Carving time: 120 hours.

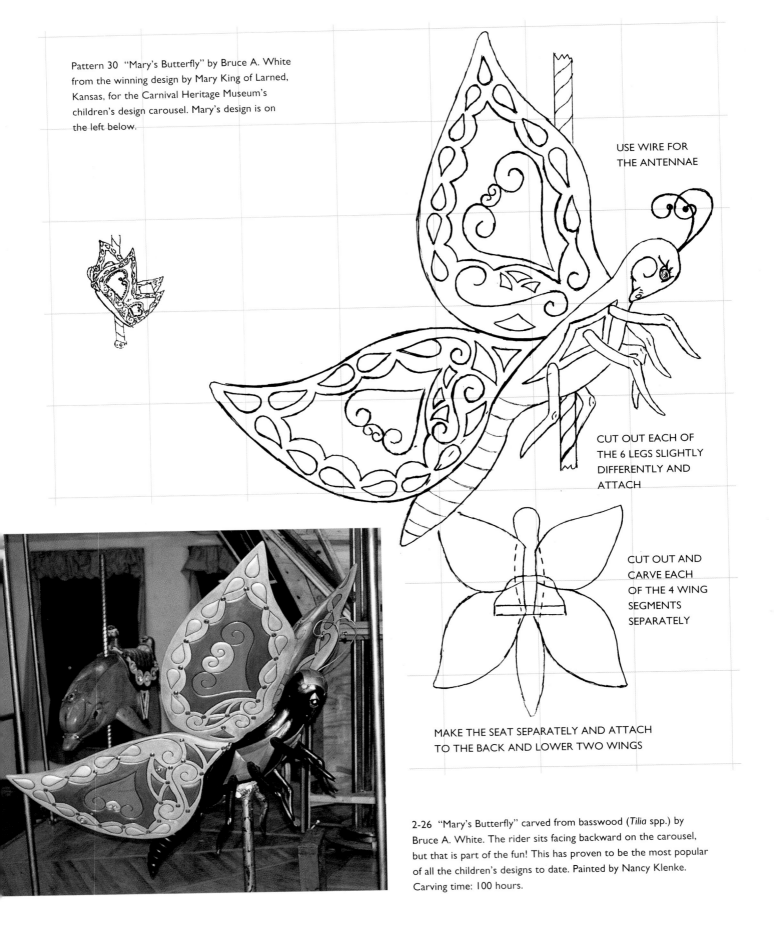

Pattern 30 "Mary's Butterfly" by Bruce A. White from the winning design by Mary King of Larned, Kansas, for the Carnival Heritage Museum's children's design carousel. Mary's design is on the left below.

USE WIRE FOR THE ANTENNAE

CUT OUT EACH OF THE 6 LEGS SLIGHTLY DIFFERENTLY AND ATTACH

CUT OUT AND CARVE EACH OF THE 4 WING SEGMENTS SEPARATELY

MAKE THE SEAT SEPARATELY AND ATTACH TO THE BACK AND LOWER TWO WINGS

2-26 "Mary's Butterfly" carved from basswood (*Tilia* spp.) by Bruce A. White. The rider sits facing backward on the carousel, but that is part of the fun! This has proven to be the most popular of all the children's designs to date. Painted by Nancy Klenke. Carving time: 100 hours.

"Jenny's Flower" winning design by Jenny Faber of Hays, Kansas, for the Carnival Heritage Museum's children's design carousel. This has not been drawn up as a pattern and completed as a carousel carving, but the estimated carving time is 60 hours. Jenny says that her favorite book as a young child was *Thumbelina*, and she had always dreamed of sitting in a flower.

Jenni Dechant of Hays, Kansas, 1997; a Seahorse designed by Mackenzie Evans of Sublette, Kansas, 1998; and a Butterfly designed by Mary King of Larned, Kansas, in 1999. They are on an operating carousel, the centerpiece of the museum.

But the dream to make a carousel honoring the master carousel carvers of the past has not been abandoned. I carve the replicas as time allows, and I have finished several, which are featured in this book along with the original creators' stories. In fact, the dream came one step closer to reality with the purchase in 1998 of the Heyn double-decker carousel frame, built circa 1900. Only seven of these antique double-decker carousel frames are known to exist. (A private collector in Germany owns the other six.) Efforts continue to raise funds to renovate the carousel frame, carve the figures for it, and build a structure to house it.

"Zach's Dragon" winning design by Zach Callaway of St. Joseph, Missouri, originally intended for the first anniversary of the "Wild Thing" carousel. This has not been drawn up as a pattern and completed as a carousel carving, but the estimated carving time is 120 hours.

Other Figures by
Bruce A. White

Other figures I have designed include "Surfer Dan, the Afghan," "Charity, the Pegasus," "Pony Express," "Tommy, the Turkey," and "Cindy, the Saltisaurus," among many others.

2-27 "Surfer Dan, the Afghan" designed and carved from cottonwood (*Populus heterophylla*) by Bruce A. White, on the "Wild Thing" carousel. The wood was chosen for the color, which closely resembles the color of a real afghan. Carving time: 25 hours.

2-28 "Charity, the Pegasus," started life as a cast copy of the "Lilly Belle" Bruce made for the Carnival Heritage Museum painted as a gray mare sporting the Missouri state flag for use on his "Wild Thing" carousel. She turned out to be the least popular figure on the carousel. Bruce's daughter Charity had always wanted him to make her a Pegasus, and finally after watching the horse go by riderless as usual he took her back to his shop, made wings for her, garbed her in new clothes, and made her a beautiful pearl white instead of the drab gray. Reintroduced to the carousel, she became an instant celebrity. She is far and away the most popular figure on his carousel among young ladies.

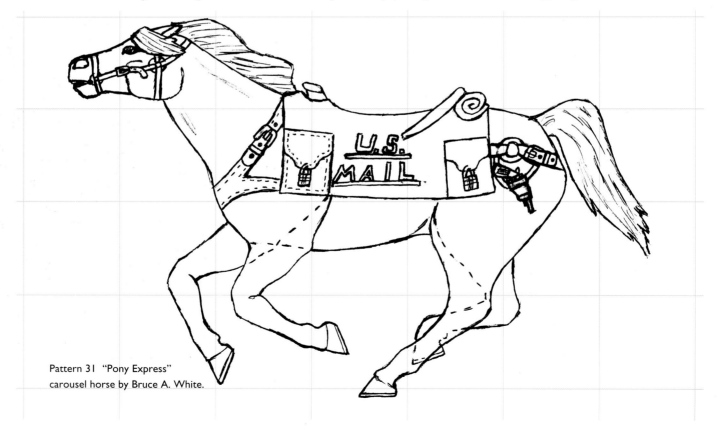

Pattern 31 "Pony Express" carousel horse by Bruce A. White.

Pattern 32 "Cindy, the Saltisaurus" dinosaur by Bruce A. White.

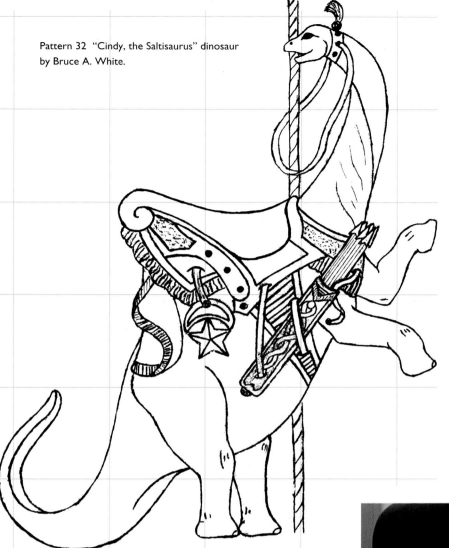

2-30 "Cindy, the Saltisaurus" dinosaur was carved from basswood (*Tilia* spp.) for a couple who lived in Hong Kong, then later moved to England. Carving time: 120 hours.

2-29 "Tommy, the Turkey" designed and carved from mulberry (*Morus* spp.) by Bruce A. White and installed on the "Wild Thing" carousel. Carving time: 120 hours.

2-31 The decor for "Cindy, the Saltisaurus" was painted by Cindy White and the rest was left natural, with a clear semi-gloss finish.

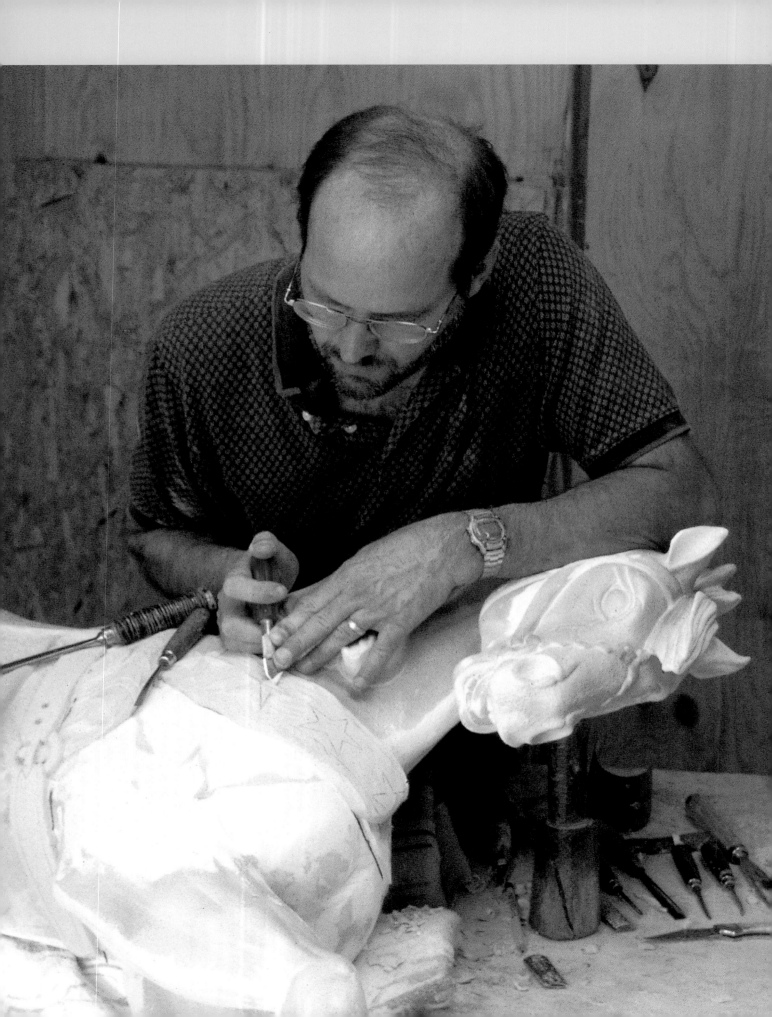

CHAPTER 3

✎ *Preparing to Carve*
a Carousel Animal

As with most projects, preparing to carve a carousel animal is mostly mental. "The proof of desire is pursuit." Of course it is helpful if you have some carving experience, but it is not essential. I would suggest that you start with a simple project, perhaps a flower carved in relief. Instructions on how to carve a rosebud, for instance, appear later on pages 130 and 131. After all, it's the same as when you carve a flower as part of a carousel horse. Then, perhaps, move on to some kind of animal carved in the round. Again, just skip ahead and follow the instructions minus the detail carving. Then wed the two together to make a carousel figure.

3-1 (FACING PAGE) Bruce is "retooling" a cast Applebee carousel horse. To sculpt the decorations, he is using a typical array of carving tools, as he would for detail carving of any wood-carved horse. These include a mallet with an assortment of gouges and chisels, a pocketknife, a file, a marker and pencil, sandpaper, and the craft knife he is using to carve the star decoration.

This horse is for a "saloon style" Applebee restaurant opening in Dodge City, Kansas. This variation is also being used in similarly themed Applebee restaurants in Texas and other locations.

You do need some equipment and space in which to work (3-1). The tools and materials are covered later in this chapter and during the actual carving in Chapter 4 of a carousel animal in miniature and in Chapter 5 of a full-size carousel animal. As for space, would you believe I do virtually all of my work in a shop that is 10 feet by 15 feet? What I don't do there, I do in my den while watching television—even the huge Stein & Goldstein figure, from Pattern 8, detailed in Chapter 5.

I will explain how you can do these projects without any of your own shop equipment and for very little money. So there's really no reason to delay any longer. Let's get started!

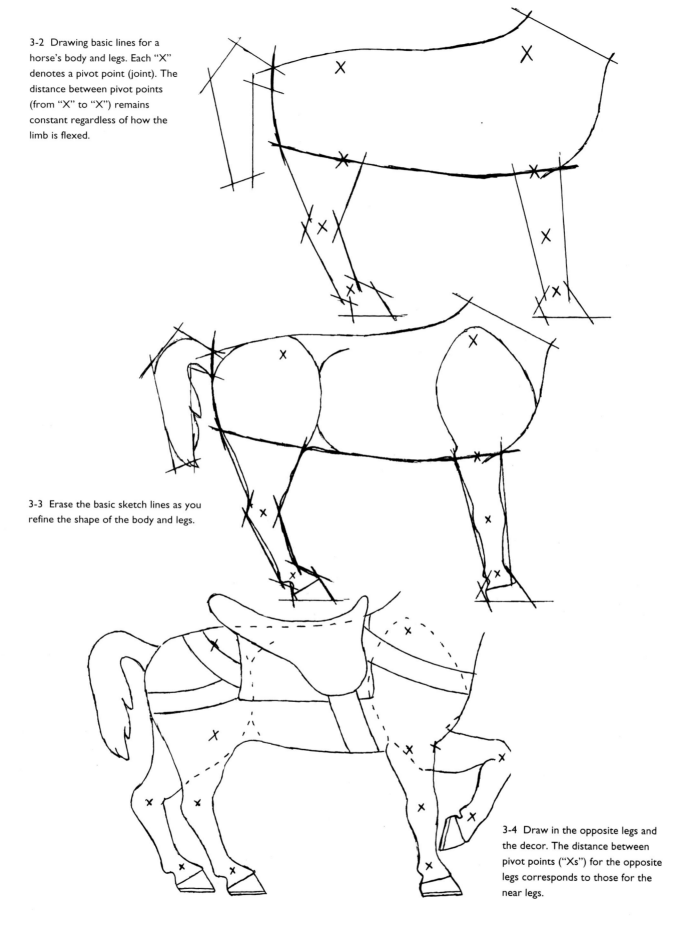

3-2 Drawing basic lines for a horse's body and legs. Each "X" denotes a pivot point (joint). The distance between pivot points (from "X" to "X") remains constant regardless of how the limb is flexed.

3-3 Erase the basic sketch lines as you refine the shape of the body and legs.

3-4 Draw in the opposite legs and the decor. The distance between pivot points ("Xs") for the opposite legs corresponds to those for the near legs.

Choosing Your Design & Planning

In this book are the stories and styles of the great carousel masters from the Golden Age of the Carousel, circa 1879–1929, in Chapter 1. Also appearing in Chapter 2 are a number of my own contemporary designs and those of my brother Brent, various clients I have had, and school-age children. From among these, you can choose one that suits your preferences and decor. Even better is if they inspire your own style and design.

You can see how to create your own design, whether a horse or a menagerie figure, by studying the patterns and photographs in this book. To create your own horse, you can start by drawing the basic lines for a horse's body and legs (3-2). Refine the shape of the hooves, legs, and tail, and sketch in the hip and shoulder (3-3). Add animation and motion to the figure by drawing in the opposite legs (3-4). You can also draw in the saddle and other desired decoration for the body of the horse.

Now you can draw the head and neck of the horse by first blocking out the basic lines (3-5). Refine the basic lines while adding the jaw line, ear, and mouth (3-6). Sketch in the mane, and the eye, nose, and mouth (3-7). Last, you can draw in the halter, bit, and any other decor (3-8).

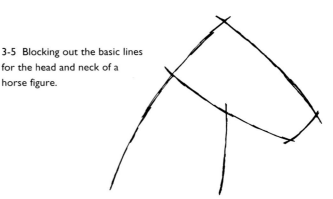

3-5 Blocking out the basic lines for the head and neck of a horse figure.

3-6 Refining the lines for the head and neck of a horse and adding basic facial features.

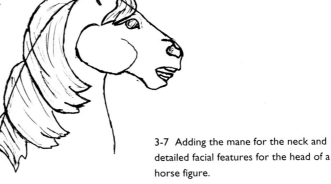

3-7 Adding the mane for the neck and detailed facial features for the head of a horse figure.

3-8 Decorating the head and neck of a horse figure with flowers and a halter and bit.

Reading through this entire book before you start may help you avoid reinventing the wheel and may save you some money as well. Whether you use a pattern from this book or choose to create your own, you may find it helpful to refer to the "rule of heads" I use to proportion a carousel horse correctly (3-9). A menagerie figure may require you to develop your own rules for proper proportion. The more familiar you are with the material in this book the better you will be able to plan your own carving and purchase the equipment and materials needed.

Miniature or Full Size? What are the Differences?

In the process of making a large or a small figure, the chief difference is the scale.

A question I often get regarding the price of a full-size carousel figure is: How much? When I tell them, I often hear, "Oh my! Well, how much for a small figure?" My answer: About the same. What most people fail to realize is that it takes me almost as long to carve a small figure as a large one, and in

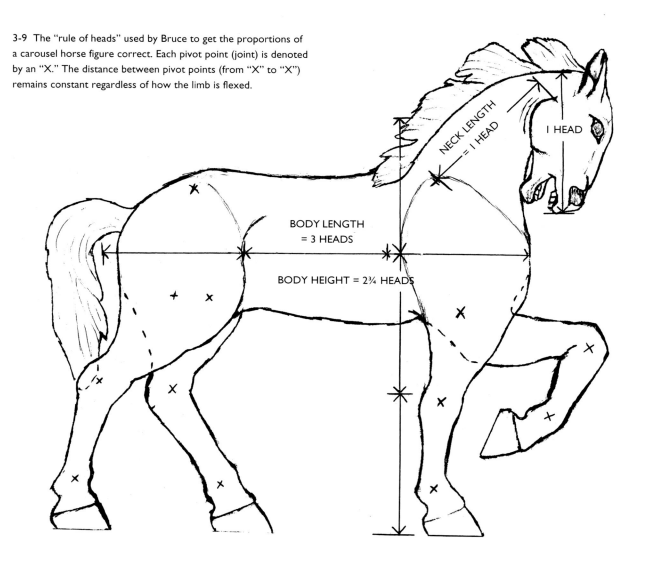

3-9 The "rule of heads" used by Bruce to get the proportions of a carousel horse figure correct. Each pivot point (joint) is denoted by an "X." The distance between pivot points (from "X" to "X") remains constant regardless of how the limb is flexed.

NECK LENGTH = 1 HEAD

1 HEAD

BODY LENGTH = 3 HEADS

BODY HEIGHT = 2¾ HEADS

some ways it is actually more difficult. I put just as much detail into a small figure as I do a large one—and believe me, it's easier to carve a larger figure. I can do a majority of the work on a large figure with power tools; I can do a lot of the fine detail by sculpting with an automotive putty, such as Bondo, which is faster than carving from wood. A small figure has to be done pretty much by hand, all the detail carved directly from the wood. And you know what? You are much more likely to cut yourself doing a small figure than a large one.

But don't let me discourage you from doing a small figure. You can do virtually all of a small figure while sitting in your easy chair watching television. A number of the steps in a large figure take a degree of physical strength—nothing a healthy adult of either gender can't handle, but if do you have a physical disability, a full-size figure may be beyond your capabilities. It's your call; large or small, each has its own rewards and challenges.

Carving Techniques & Decorative Work

Ultimately, you must develop your own carving techniques, of course. But there are some definite do's and don'ts and I have a lot of tricks and secrets. Most of these are explained in my instructions for carving a miniature figure, but some that are more specific to large pieces will be found in Chapter 5, in the section on Carving & Sculpting Techniques. There is some crossover in techniques and decorative work for large and small figures, so you might find it advantageous to read through both Chapters 4 and 5 before starting a figure of any size. The most basic principle to keep in mind is that carving with the grain is always desirable. I call this carving "downhill" so that I am always aware of the direction of the grain (3-10). With the proper tool, such as a gouge, you can also comfortably carve across the grain (3-11).

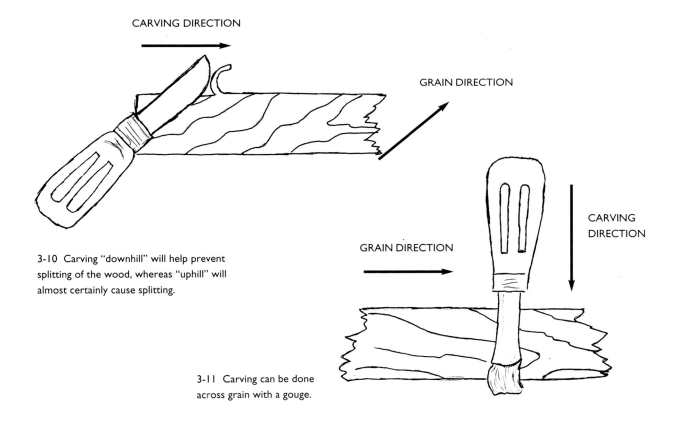

CARVING DIRECTION

GRAIN DIRECTION

3-10 Carving "downhill" will help prevent splitting of the wood, whereas "uphill" will almost certainly cause splitting.

GRAIN DIRECTION

CARVING DIRECTION

3-11 Carving can be done across grain with a gouge.

Sculpting with Putty

First let me do a little defining. All carving was once included in the word "sculpture," which appeared in the late Middle Ages based on the Latin word for "to carve." The English word "carve" has Germanic origins meaning to shape artistically by cutting or chiseling. The term sculpture has come to be associated with fine art and the production of figures in the round. Whereas carving is limited to the act of taking material away, i.e., reducing the material on which the artist works, sculpting includes the act of adding to and molding material to achieve a desired form. It is thus that I distinguish between carving—that is, cutting or chiseling (3-12)—and sculpting, which I use to refer to molding (3-13), a proper part of its usage through the ages.

Wood artists in the United States refer to themselves as "wood sculptors," which is technically correct in the broader sense of "sculpting," but to my mind they are carvers. I use both carving

and molding in my work. I cover carving extensively in Chapter 4, with some specific techniques in Chapter 5, so here I offer a brief summary of how I mold, or sculpt.

I use primarily automotive putty (Bondo, or another similar product), which is a fiberglass derivative. The way I use it, it can be regarded as a chemically reactive clay. The putty comes as a relatively stiff material, with the approximate viscosity of thick molasses. Adding a very small amount of the hardener causes the putty to react, becoming hard in 5 to 10 minutes.

3-12 Bruce can be seen doing some of the detail carving for the Illions-style flower horse, Pattern 7.

3-13 A close-up of the head of the Illions-style flower horse from Pattern 7 shows the use of automotive putty, the tannish-white areas, for sculpting as needed.

As manufactured, automotive putty has a couple of problems that curtail its usefulness for my particular application. It is not thick enough and it reacts (hardens) too quickly. I solve the first problem by mixing in sawdust until the material is the desired consistency, approximating that of clay. I solve the second problem by keeping the mixture refrigerated. The colder the material is, the more slowly it reacts. I also try to work in a cool area. On a hot day, or in a hot workshop, you won't have much working time.

Drill holes at eccentric angles into the wood under where you are going to add the material; make the holes of a size appropriate to what you are going to sculpt onto your figure. Add the hardener to your pre-mixed putty/sawdust mixture and combine them thoroughly. You must work quickly. Mix only a small portion at a time. You can see more on how this is done by following through the section "Carving & Sculpting Techniques" in Chapter 5, on pages 129 through 132.

Press your putty/sawdust mix into the drilled holes and roughly model the material into the shape you want. Use your fingers and sculpting tools to do this, or use your carving tools as sculpting tools. Since the automotive putty is oil-based, it will not harm your tools. Sculpt only a small area at a time. For example, if you are doing a spray of five flowers, rough sculpt only one flower at a time (3-14). The putty/sawdust mix will seam-lessly adhere to itself even if the first area is already cured.

The putty/sawdust clay, since it is chemically reactive, will get mildly hot as it reacts while being applied. When it has cooled to the touch, you can do the refining and detail shaping, carving the material just as you do wood. You will find that this material, while rather hard, carves extremely well and will accept paint evenly so that the carved wood and sculpted putty/sawdust mix are no longer distinguishable (3-15).

3-14 In the making of the Dentzel-style "Blue Ribbon Betsy" carousel horse from Pattern 2, Bruce has made extensive use of automotive putty for sculpting the decorations. I. D. Looff used a similar method of applying decoration, first casting rosettes and small flowers from plaster and then attaching them to the carving.

3-15 As Bruce's daughter, Charity White Saddler, paints the Dentzel-style "Blue Ribbon Betsy" carousel horse from Pattern 2, the sculpted automotive putty can no longer be distinguished from the carved wood.

Tools & Materials

I cannot stress enough that, when it comes to woodworking tools in general and carving tools in particular, you really do get what you pay for. If you buy inexpensive tools, they will almost invariably be of poor quality. Inexpensive power tools will have a short life span, vibrate badly, and often get hot. Inexpensive knives, chisels, and gouges will not have the razor sharp edges you need, and if you do manage to get a good edge on them, it will not hold.

A good band saw is a necessity. If you do not have one and are unwilling to invest in one, perhaps you can find someone who does, and is willing to let you use it, or will do the cut-out for you. Many colleges and community centers have woodworking shops you can access for a small fee.

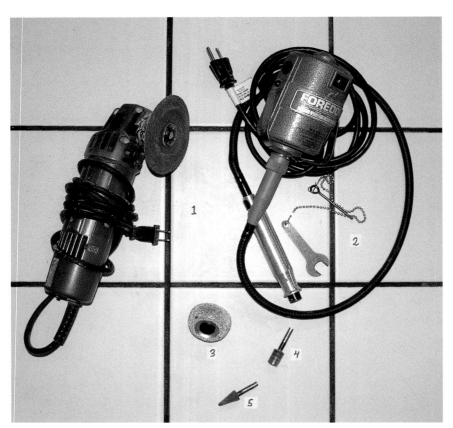

3-16 Power tools for rough shaping and bulk wood removal. Numbers for specific tools are described in the text.

Power Tools for a Small Figure

For a small figure, the pictured power tools are the only ones really needed. I use them only for bulk wood removal/rough shaping (3-16). The following numbers correspond to the numbers for the power tools for rough shaping and bulk wood removal in 3-16.

1. Angle grinder with a sanding disk attachment. Use a coarse grit sanding disk. This setup will remove wood very quickly. Be very careful if you lose control of the tool; the edge of the disk will cut you like a knife.

2. A rotary tool. A word of caution: I do not recommend a rotary tool in which the motor is in the hand piece. I don't care what the advertisements say; they will vibrate. If you use it for very long, your hand will start to get numb. These tools also tend to get hot. The one pictured is made by Foredom, which I recommend. This is the brand that is used in hospitals for surgery and autopsies. The motor hangs separately. The hand piece is attached to the motor by a flexible shaft. You can run it at a constant speed through the on/off switch or hook it up to a variable speed foot pedal. It fits various size collets, which allows for bits ranging from extremely small to large.

3. A "wood blaster" attachment is very good for removing a lot of material in a hurry for a small project. But be very careful. This large an attachment on your

hand piece will generate a lot of torque. It can get away from you or tear the part you are working on right out of your hand. I suggest clamping the part down and using both hands to hold the hand piece.

4. and 5. Large, coarse burrs. These are also good for rapid wood removal, when you are getting closer to your target lines.

Tools for Detail Carving

For detail carving, hand knives, chisels, and gouges work much better than power tools, allowing for much cleaner cuts (3-17). The following numbers correspond to the numbers for the sharpening stones, hand knives, chisels, and gouges for detail carving in 3-17.

1. Grinding stones, coarse and smooth. It takes a little practice to get a razor edge, but you will master it in a short time. Just relax, disconnect your mind from it, and let your hands do the work while you watch television or read a book. Practice will allow you to master and keep the right angle as you hone your tools. Use a circular motion with light to medium pressure. Use the coarse stone first, if the tool is dull, then obtain the razor edge with the fine stone. Once you get a razor edge, I suggest you maintain it with frequent use of the fine or "slick" stone.

2. A good pocket knife with a blade approximately 3 to 4 inches long. You will be surprised how much you use this tool.

3. X-Acto craft knife with a No. 2 disposable blade. You'll find this especially useful for fine detail on a small figure.

4. X-Acto craft knife with a No. 22 disposable blade. I use this tool on small figures far more than any other. The disposable blades are razor sharp and inexpensive. When one starts to lose its razor edge, I just dispose of it and put in a new one. It saves a lot of time. The No. 22 blade is a very good general-purpose blade.

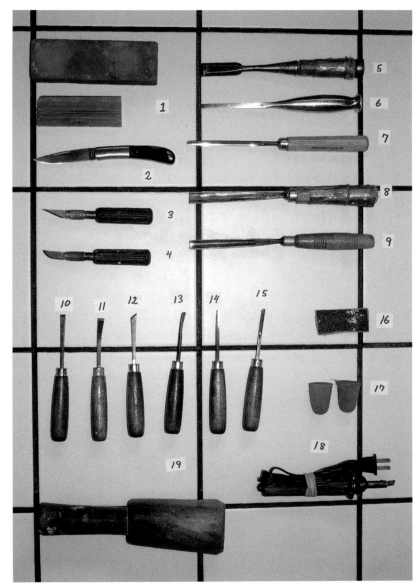

3-17 Sharpening stones, hand knives, chisels, and gouges for detail carving. Numbers for specific tools are described in the text.

5. This is a 1-inch straight chisel. I use this tool most often for large figures, but occasionally on small ones. I use this one a lot for rough shaping.

6. This is a ¼-inch straight chisel, as above. Mine was an orthopedic surgery chisel, cast off because it had a small scratch on it. If you know any operating room technicians, ask them to keep an eye out for orthopedic surgical gouges and chisels that can no longer be used in the surgical operating room. There are no better carving tools. Use it for rough shaping.

7. This is a ¼-inch gouge. Used primarily for large figures, but occasionally for small ones as well. Used for rough shaping.

8. This is a 1-inch gouge, as above. As you may have guessed, this is my favorite and most commonly used tool for large figures. I use it for rough shaping.

9. V tool, also called a parting tool. I use this a lot on both large and small figures. This tool is used for the initial cuts along the lines you draw for your decorations after the rough shaping is done, or for carving hair flow lines.

10. to 15. Palm tools or detail tools. These are essential for carving small figures and you will be using them extensively, so be sure you invest in good ones. They can generally be purchased as a set.

Number 10 is a ¼-inch straight chisel.

Number 11 is a ¼-inch straight bent chisel.

Number 12 is a ¼-inch skew chisel.

Number 13 is a ¼-inch gouge.

Number 14 is a ⅛-inch gouge.

Number 15 is a V or parting tool.

16. Sander. You had better get skilled at operating this tool, because you will be using it a lot. I recommend you use a closed coat, cloth-backed sandpaper. It costs more than regular sandpaper, but will last much longer. I buy sanding

❧ Helpful Accessories

If you suffer from arthritis in your hands, you may want to use a power, reciprocating hand piece (not pictured in 3-17), which will hold various gouges and chisels, for the rough shaping. I actually like them better than rotary tools, because you will avoid the dust, but they aren't as fast as a rotary tool or a professional carver with mallet and chisels.

Metal mesh or fillet glove. Found in most sporting goods stores in the fishing section. I strongly recommend you purchase one of these if you are a beginning carver. Wear it on the hand you use to hold your figure while carving. It can prevent your getting blood on your figure, which can be very annoying, especially since it is yours.

Elastic wrist brace. This is especially important if you suffer from arthritis or will carve for long periods at a time. Wear it on your working hand.

belts intended for use with belt sanders and cut them into small, easily handled pieces. Keep 40 grit, 80 grit and 120 grit on hand. The 40 and 80 grit I actually use to do some of the shaping. I use the 120 grit for finish sanding.

17. Rubber finger protectors. You will appreciate these when you start sanding your figure.

18. Wood burning pen. An easier way of putting in flow lines than carving, especially if you are using a hard wood or wood with a difficult grain. This is also very useful when incising a lot of lines across grain, close together, such as for fringe on blankets.

19. Mallet. Used in rough shaping. You probably won't need this for a small figure, but you may. On a large figure, it will save a lot of wear and tear on your wrists and elbows when removing a lot of wood with chisels and gouges.

Additional Tools Needed for a Full-size Figure

When you decide to carve a full-size figure, a few additional tools will be useful, including a carbide grinder wheel, a "supercut" grinding wheel, a reciprocating saw, and a small, electric chainsaw. You can see these in use in Chapter 5, where I demonstrate full-size carving.

No additional hand tools are needed other than those listed above for small projects, since you are doing the bulk wood removal with these tools.

A carbide grinder wheel for wood is a very handy angle grinder attachment that can remove a lot of wood in a hurry. Be sure to wear sturdy leather gloves and use both hands when using this tool. You can buy this attachment in a number of configurations and coarsenesses. Since you will use it for bulk wood removal, I recommend the coarse, donut wheel.

The "supercut" is another tool similar to the carbide wood grinder wheel by which a lot of large project carvers swear. It is essentially a chainsaw on a 4-inch wheel, that attaches to your angle grinder.

Obviously, this tool can be very dangerous; appropriate caution must be taken.

A reciprocating saw, using a coarse-cut, 6-inch blade, is used to cut down close to the lines you have drawn for the front and back profiles on the legs and tail. Do not try to cut right along the lines. If you do, you will likely get a skewed cut, and ruin your piece. Cut approximately one-half inch outside of your line, then use your wood grinding wheel or "supercut" attachment to remove the rest of the wood down to your lines. Also use your reciprocating saw to cut down the corners for the head/neck and torso.

A small, electric chainsaw is very useful when doing large projects. However, I do *not* recommend this tool unless you have a lot of experience with it for conventional use. A chainsaw can be extremely dangerous if you are not in full control of it at all times. It can cause serious, even deadly, injury. The results that I can obtain with the chainsaw can be achieved just as satisfactorily with the other power tools that I have described—just not quite as quickly.

CHAPTER 4

◟ *Carving Your Own Carousel Animal in Miniature*

"The Creator gathered in His hands the southern wind.

Breathing life, He said, 'To you I give flight without wings.'"

—*derived from a Bedouin myth for the creation of the horse*

We can never hope even to approach the beauty and grace which our Creator imparts to all of his creations, but if you will allow me, I'll show you how I make a carousel figure. In this chapter I'll show you how I carve in miniature the parade horse, pattern 8, designed by Stein & Goldstein, circa 1912 (4-1). Then in Chapter 5, I'll show how to carve this same pattern, which is one of the largest standers made, in full size. Painting details will be covered as well..

4-1 (FACING PAGE) Bruce is working on the assembled miniature figure of the parade horse, pattern 8, carving the details. Carving a carousel horse in miniature from this Stein & Goldstein pattern is shown in successive steps in this chapter.

Approaching the Project One Step at a Time

Taken as a whole, the project can seem overwhelming. If you limit your focus to each step, one step at a time, as I take you through it, the whole process will be simpler and easier to understand. You've selected a carousel pattern to carve, gathered some tools, and have your wood at hand. If you're not an experienced carver, don't panic. Keep in mind that carving a carousel animal proceeds one step at a time. Start by familiarizing yourself with equine anatomy and accouterments on the next page.

Step 1. I suggest you enlarge the pattern to at least 12-inches, preferably 18-inches, wide. This may be a little bigger than you had in mind, but especially if you are a beginner, it is the optimal size. Read through Step 2, and then cut the pattern, cutting out the individual body parts (4-2).

Be sure to label the legs on the pattern. Cut both right legs out first. Trace them on another sheet of paper. Tape them back onto the pattern, then cut both left legs out along the dotted lines. An X-Acto knife with either a No. 2 or No. 22 blade works best.

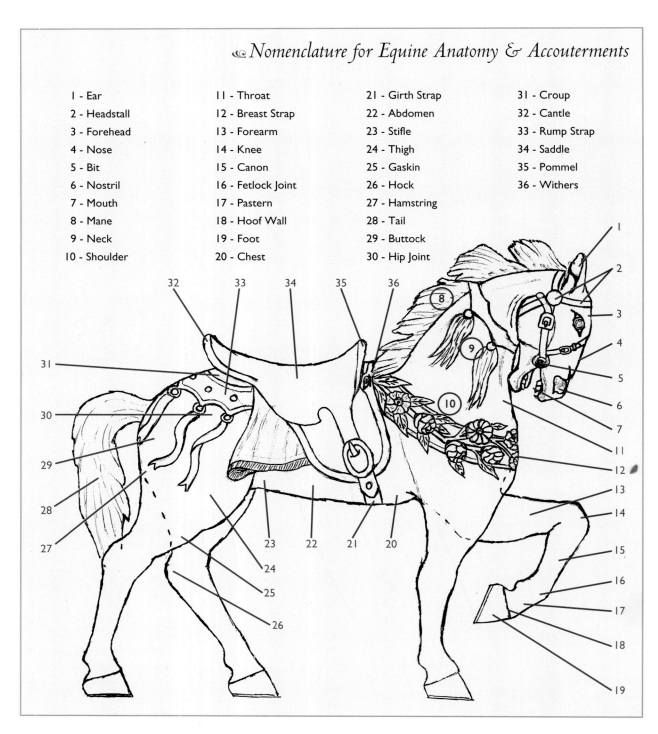

Nomenclature for Equine Anatomy & Accouterments

1 - Ear
2 - Headstall
3 - Forehead
4 - Nose
5 - Bit
6 - Nostril
7 - Mouth
8 - Mane
9 - Neck
10 - Shoulder

11 - Throat
12 - Breast Strap
13 - Forearm
14 - Knee
15 - Canon
16 - Fetlock Joint
17 - Pastern
18 - Hoof Wall
19 - Foot
20 - Chest

21 - Girth Strap
22 - Abdomen
23 - Stifle
24 - Thigh
25 - Gaskin
26 - Hock
27 - Hamstring
28 - Tail
29 - Buttock
30 - Hip Joint

31 - Croup
32 - Cantle
33 - Rump Strap
34 - Saddle
35 - Pommel
36 - Withers

Using Your Pattern

Step 2. After you have cut out the pattern, lay the pieces on the wood and trace onto the wood (4-3). Pay attention to the direction of the wood grain, as shown in (4-4). This matters even for a small figure. Running the grain in the proper direction not only ensures strength for your figure, but makes it much easier to carve. I suggest you use 2-inch-thick wood; preferably, Honduran mahogany (*Swietenia macrophylla*), basswood (*Tilia* spp.), or white pine (*Pinus strobus*). You can use any wood you want, but these are woods that are relatively soft and have an even, consistent grain.

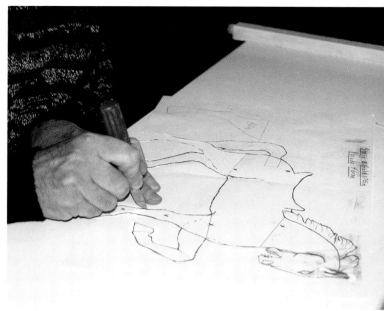

4-2 Cutting out the pattern.

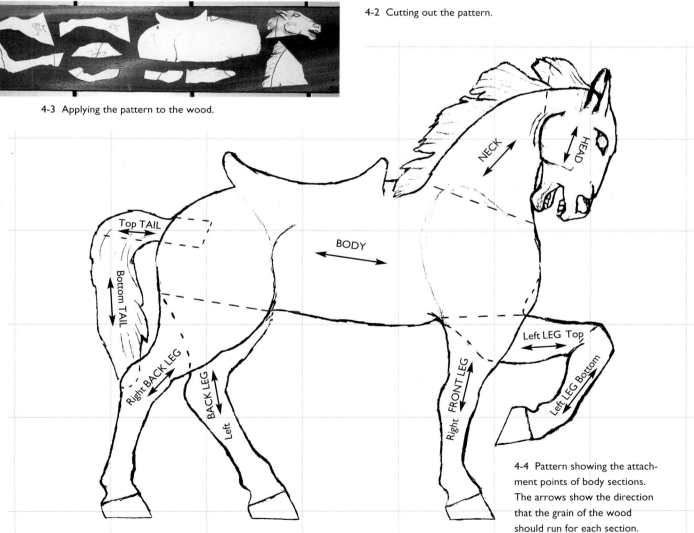

4-3 Applying the pattern to the wood.

4-4 Pattern showing the attachment points of body sections. The arrows show the direction that the grain of the wood should run for each section.

Harder or softer woods each present their own sets of problems, which you can avoid by using the above-mentioned woods. If using 2-inch-thick wood, cut each leg and the tail out once, the body, neck, and head twice. Cut one of your two head and neck sections in half. Cut one-half off of each leg. Cut the tail in half. You will be gluing together two, 2-inch-thick sections for the body, for a total of 4 inches. You will be gluing together 1½-inch-thick sections for the neck and 1½-inch-thick sections for the head so that both sections, when glued together, will be 3-inches thick. Each leg will be 1-inch thick; the tail 1-inch thick. Be sure to label your parts.

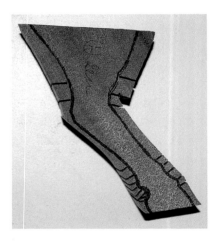

4-5 Cut-out section with relief cuts for cutting to shape on the band saw.

Step 3. Cut the sections apart on a band saw. Make relief cuts so the band saw blade won't bind when you cut the pieces to shape (4-5).

Step 4. Cut the pieces to shape and to proper thickness (4-6). I advise that you use a band saw. If you try to use a hand-held jigsaw for 2-inch-thick wood, you will have skewed cuts. And since the parts are small, you may also soon be missing some fingers.

Step 5. Glue and clamp the parts you need to laminate (4-7). Use a good-quality PVA (polyvinyl acetate) glue. Elmer's or Tightbond wood glue will both work very well. Be sure to spread the glue over the entire surface. Don't assume it will spread by itself when it's clamped, because it won't. Be sure the surfaces being glued together are mirror-smooth and flat. If the boards have been run through a planer, they will be. If you don't have a planer, most dealers in hardwood will plane the boards for you for a small charge. Use "C" clamps to clamp these parts together for at least 12 hours.

4-6 Sections cut to shape and proper thickness.

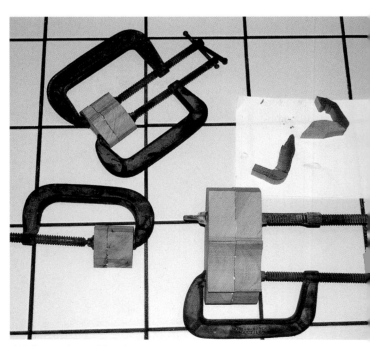

4-7 Pieces clamped for gluing.

When gluing the two pieces of the bent leg (the left leg) and the two pieces of the tail together, make sure the parts being glued together are mirror-smooth and fit perfectly flush together. If this is not the case, you will not achieve a good glue bond. If it is, the glue bond will be stronger than the wood. For a small, decorative figure, you can put the glue on the parts to be joined, spread the glue, and press together, holding them tightly for about 5 minutes. Lay the piece on a flat surface and do not disturb for at least 12 hours. Do not use super glue for this procedure. You will get a superior bond with wood glue.

Drawing in the Contours

Step 7. After the glued parts are dry, draw in the contours. First, find your centerline; draw it in. For the tail, do not make the centerline a straight line. Rather, have it waver a bit from side to side. This will give the tail motion and thus impart motion to the entire figure. For the head, neck and body, the centerline is straight—straight down the center. For the body, you can give the centerline a slight curve if you want to give the appearance that your figure is bending a bit. However, if you are a beginner, I would not recommend this. Remember, each part will have bilateral symmetry from each view (4-8). Once you have your centerline drawn in for each part, draw one side, then just copy its mirror image on the other side of your centerline.

For the front legs, front profile, note that the centerline angles from the center at the top to just off center at the hoof (4-9). Off center to the right for the right leg; to the left for the left leg. It is the same width at the bottom of the hoof, at the hoof wall, at the fetlock joint, and at the knee. The hoof is very slightly narrower than the hoof wall where they (the hoof and the hoof wall) meet, at the top. The pastern is slightly narrower than the hoof wall and fetlock joint. The canon is narrowest just above the fetlock joint, then widens gradually to the knee joint. The forearm is narrowest just above the knee joint. Note that the forearm joins the torso differently on the shoulder than it does to the chest.

For the back leg, front profile draw a centerline as you did for the front leg (4-10). Draw the same as the front leg from the bottom of the hoof to the fetlock joint. For the inside of the leg, a very gently concave line to the hock joint, then very gently convex for the gaskin and thigh, then gently concave into the belly. For the outside of the

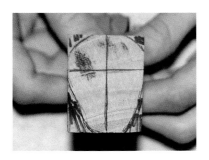

4-8 Contours are symmetrical.

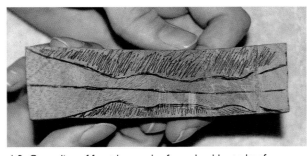

4-9 Centerline of front legs angles from shoulder to hoof.

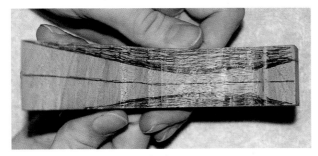

4-10 Back leg contours from the front.

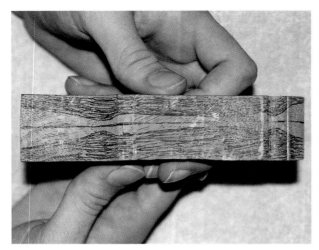

4-11 Back leg contours from the back.

4-12 Top of the head contours.

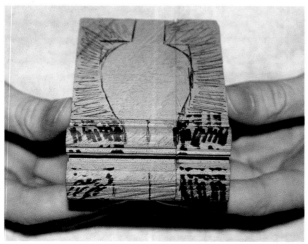

4-13 Head contours from chin to back.

leg, a gently concave line to the hock joint, then gently convex for the gaskin and thigh. The back profile is much narrower than front profile, and should be drawn as in (4-11).

For the head, start with a simple wedge shape from the top, the narrowest point being at the nose, the widest, the forehead across the eyes (4-12). From the forehead, draw a straight line to where the head joins the neck. From the bottom, make the chin slightly narrower than across the top of the nose (4-13). For the ears, the outside edge can be continuous with the head/neck, or flare out, depending on the attitude you want to give the ears. After the outside edge is drawn, draw the inside edges as shown.

For the neck, draw a very gentle arcing line on the back from where the neck joins the head to where the neck joins the body (4-14). If the mane is flowing over the neck, be sure to draw it a little wider where the mane is flowing. For the throat, draw it slightly more narrow than back. Draw an oval, as shown (4-15), on the top of the neck where the neck joins the head and on the bottom where the neck joins the body.

4-14 Neck contours allowing for the mane.

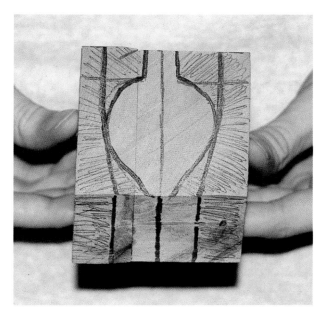

4-15 Oval contour where neck joins the head.

To ensure that you are drawing a good mirror image of the first side you drew, and to keep equidistant on both sides of the centerline, use a small ruler, preferably in metric measurements, since they are in smaller increments. When drawing the second side, measure from the centerline an equal distance on both sides every few centimeters, making dash marks (4-18). Then connect the dashes.

4-17 Using an undulating centerline on the tail piece.

For the body, draw a straight line equidistant from each side of your centerline (4-16).

For the tail, start narrowest from where the tail joins the body, flare out slightly where the tail curls downward (this is the widest point on your tail), and taper down to a rounded point at the top of the tail (4-17).

4-16 Marking the body section.

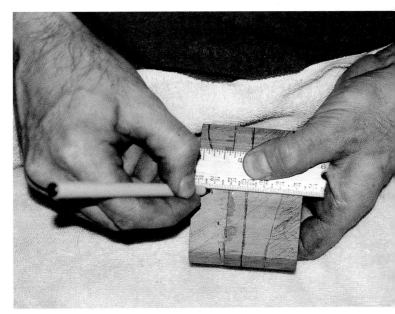

4-18 Using a ruler to mark the mirror-image contour.

Carving the Parts

Step 8. Now that you have the front and back profiles of the body parts drawn, start blocking them out by cutting away the bulk of the wood to the lines you have drawn (4-19 to 4-22). Much of it can be removed with a band saw. Do not cut with the band saw right along the lines you have drawn. If you do, you will have a skewed cut and a ruined part. You should be careful to cut down just close to them; the object being to have less wood to remove by hand. If you have a rotary tool with a large, coarse burr bit, remove the rest with it. If not, finish the blocking out with a craft knife, large gouge, or straight chisel. Do not round off yet.

When blocking out the parts, with a craft knife, note the two different carving grips. In the first, you hold the knife handle in the curl of your fingers with the blade edge toward you (4-23). Brace your thumb against the end of the part you are working on. Pull your fingers back toward your palm. Use this grip whenever possible. It gives you the best leverage and control, and is therefore the safest.

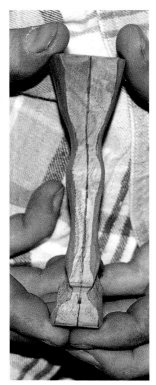
4-19 Front leg blocked out, seen from the front.

4-20 Front leg blocked out, seen from the back.

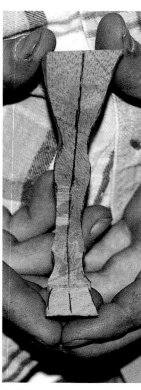
4-21 Back leg blocked out, seen from the front.

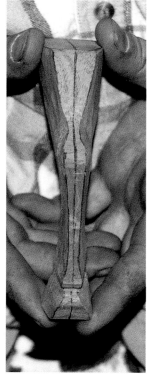
4-22 Back leg blocked out, seen from the back.

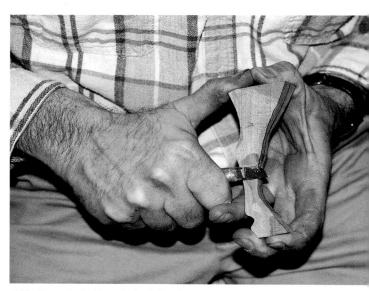
4-23 First grip, holding the knife handle in the curl of your fingers with the blade edge toward you, and bracing your thumb against the end of the part you are working on.

In the second grip, you are carving away from you (4-24). Hold the knife handle in the curl of your fingers, the blade edge pointing away from you, your thumb braced against the haft. Hold the part you are working on in the fingers and palm of your other hand. Use the thumb of the hand holding the part to help push and guide the blade during the cut.

You can use a ⅛-inch palm gouge to cut across grain to form the pastern (4-25).

Rounding Off the Edges

Step 9. Draw in your centerline for the side profiles (4-26). Note that the "center" line should actually be a little off center, towards the front of the leg. Round over the edges of the legs from centerline side profiles to centerline front and back profiles (4-27). For a small figure, you will find that the No. 22 X-Acto craft knife blade or a sharp pocketknife works best.

4-24 Second grip, holding the knife handle in the curl of your fingers, the blade edge pointing away from you, your thumb braced against the handle.

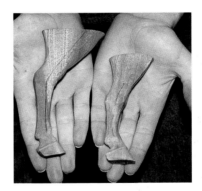

4-26 Draw the centerlines for each piece, noting that they are intentionally slightly off-center.

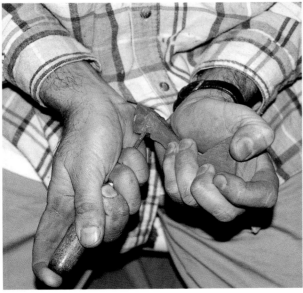

4-25 Using a ⅛-inch palm gouge to cut across grain to form the pastern.

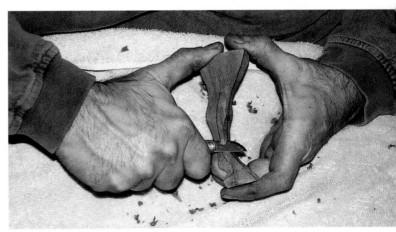

4-27 Roughing out the edges of a leg piece.

You will start to carve the hoof wall at this point. Make a stop cut in along the hoof wall line, with the edge of the knife. Press down hard with the edge of the blade, starting at the back of the blade, then roll the blade forward, toward the tip, keeping firm pressure. Then bevel in, carving from the bottom of the hoof toward the hoof wall. Do not round over the back of the hoof below this line. Do not forget about bilateral symmetry when rounding over and forming the hoof and hoof wall.

Step 10. After you have finished rounding off and forming the hoof wall and hoof, sand the areas smooth. Nothing fancy; you aren't done carving yet, just sand off the rough edges and angles (4-28, 4-29). On the tail, let your creative juices flow and just do some freeform shaping and then carve in the hair flow lines. Use the large V tool first for the occasional deeper folds (4-30). Use the small V tool to carve in the hair flow. Use 80-grit sandpaper to sand smooth.

Adding Details

Step 11. Draw in the details for the legs—joints, muscles, tendons, the frog (i.e., the bottom and back of hoof), and horseshoe (4-31, 4-32). Carve out the shaded areas (4-33). You do not

4-28 Legs roughed out and rough sanded, side view.

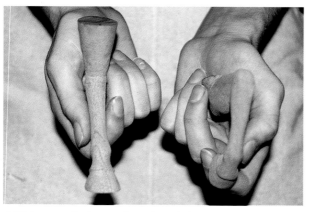

4-29 Legs roughed out and rough sanded, front view.

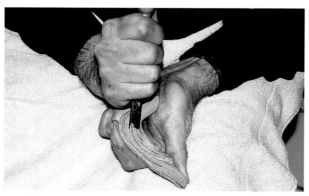

4-30 The tail is roughed out and sanded smooth, then hair flow lines are drawn in and then carved with V tools.

necessarily need to carve out the frog on the hooves of the legs on which the horse is standing, since it is not easily "seen"; however, the mark of a master craftsman is attention to detail. In countries where carving is very highly regarded and considered a fine art, such as Japan and Germany, the first areas to be examined for craftsmanship are those not normally seen.

To form the frog and bottom of the horseshoe, use the tip of the No. 22 blade to incise along the horseshoe line and the outside edge of the frog (4-34). Roll the edge of the No. 22 blade down the center of the frog on the bottom of the hoof and around to the center of the back of the hoof. Use the ⅛-inch gouge or knife edge to carve out the bottom of the hoof between the horseshoe and the outside edge of the frog (4-35). Use the No. 22 blade or your pocketknife to carve out the inside of the frog.

To form the horseshoe, roll the edge of the No. 22 blade along the horseshoe line to form the stop cut (4-36). Carve out shaded area.

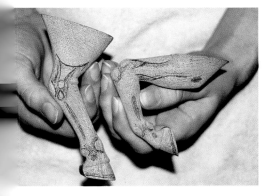

4-31 Draw in the details for the frog (i.e., the bottom and back of hoof) and horseshoe.

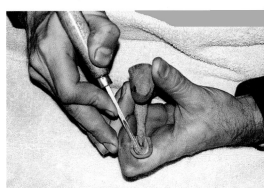

4-34 Using the tip of the No. 22 blade to incise along the horseshoe line and the outside edge of the frog.

4-32 Draw in the details for the joints, muscles, and tendons of the legs.

4-35 Using the ⅛-inch gouge to carve out the bottom of the hoof between the horseshoe and the outside edge of the frog.

4-33 Use the ⅛-inch gouge to carve out the shaded areas to form the joints, muscles, and tendons.

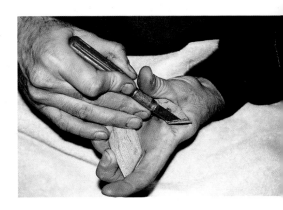

4-36 Forming the horseshoe by rolling the No. 22 blade along the horseshoe line to form the stop cut.

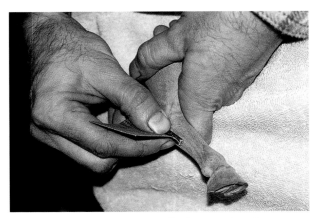

4-37 Roll the sandpaper into a small tube to sand out between the muscles, tendons, and other similar areas.

Step 12. Sand the pieces using closed coat sanding belts intended for belt sanders, cut into smaller pieces. This type of sand "paper" is stiffer than the more commonly used sandpaper and is ideal for shaping, especially for smaller figures such as those on which we are working. The edge can be used to sand out the edge of the horseshoe and other areas that have sharp inside corners. Fold the sandpaper in half to form a tight radius edge to sand between the knee joints, inside the frog, and other similar areas. Roll the sandpaper into a small tube to sand out between the muscles, tendons, and other similar areas (4-37).

Carving the Neck & Head

Step 13. Draw in the arch of the neck/mane. Since this is a "flyaway" mane, it is easier to carve than a mane that flows over the neck and is thus a good figure for practice. Also draw in the ear and curve of the jaw (4-38).

Carve the shaded areas out to form the mane and arch of the neck (4-39). The cylinder burr with a rotary tool is a good tool with which to carve this. Be sure to wear a dust mask when using the rotary tool. If you do not have a rotary tool, carve out using a ½-inch or ¼-inch gouge. Draw the "center" line back in for the mane as shown, but don't make it straight—that's boring. Wave it back and forth.

Start rounding off and shaping the neck, rounding over from "center" line to center-line (4-40). Your sharp pocketknife or X-Acto No. 22 blade works best for this step. Round the mane over to the centerline.

Draw in the eye set and nostril set for the head (4-41). You must get them correct first and round out and shape the rest of the head around them. First carve the nostril set and draw in the nostril. For carousel horses in most styles, the nostril is shaped

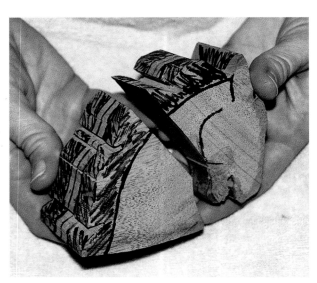

4-38 Draw in the mane as well as the ear and curve of the jaw.

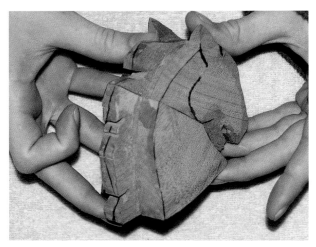

4-39 Carve arch of the neck and the mane and then redraw the "center" line back in for the mane as shown, allowing it to wave back and forth.

4-40 The neck and mane roughed out along the weaving "center" line.

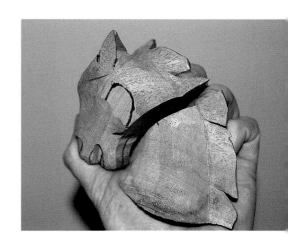

4-42 The back of the head and neck are carved and rounded from the centerline to the mane and up to the back of the ear.

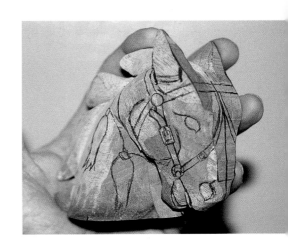

4-41 The eye set and nostril set are drawn in and carved out before you round out and shape the rest of the head around them.

Step 14. With most of the rounding off done, this is a good time to glue the neck and head together. Turn the head on the neck a bit to help give animation and motion. Let dry for at least 12 hours.

Adding Decoration

Step 15. Draw in the eye, headstall, and other decoration (4-43). For the eye, be careful not to draw it up too high. You need to leave enough room for the eyelid and brow. Do not draw the eye parallel to the forehead. This is a very common error. The back corner should be pointed midway between the bottom of the ear and the angle of the jaw.

like a modified numeral "6." For Dare, Armitage-Herschell, and Parker figures, it is a simple oval. Make sure you have it angled correctly and that the nostrils are level with each other from both the front and top profiles. Carve out the eye set. Don't get too carried away yet. Leave enough wood to carve the headstall and any other decoration. The ¼-inch palm gouge works best. Carve out wood from below the ear, between the eye set line, and cheek line, and around the nostril.

Carve out the back of the head, rounding from your centerline to the mane and up to the back of the ear (4-42). Round off the front of the muzzle, around the nostril. After you have rounded off the front of the muzzle, draw in the teeth and tongue. Round off slightly the bottom of the chin and jaw. Carve out the rest of the mane on the back of the head.

4-43 The eye, headstall, and other decoration is drawn.

You might want to cut a pattern for the eye to ensure they are the same size and shape. When drawing in the eyes, check carefully that they are at the same level and angle. Also, be sure to draw them a little larger than you want the finished eyes to be. The eyes will appear smaller when carved than they do in the drawing.

Carve out the angle of the jaw and round over the forehead. Carve out around the headstall and other decoration. Do not carve out the details of the eyes, nostrils, mouth, or ears before each of these is roughed out (4-44).

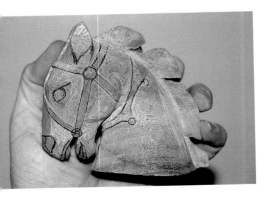

4-44 Carve out around the headstall and other decoration, carve out the angle of the jaw, and round over the forehead. The details of the eyes, nostrils, mouth, and ears are not carved before each of these is roughed out.

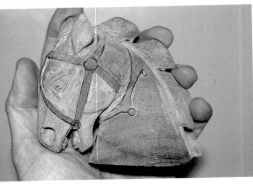

4-45 The details of the head and neck are carved out, seen from the left side.

4-46 The mane hair flow is carved out and sanded along with the other details of the head and neck, seen from the right side.

Finishing the Head Details

Step 16. Now you are ready to finish the details for the head and neck (4-45). Before carving the ears, decide in what attitude you want the ears to be. Horses' ears have a remarkable range of motion; they can turn in virtually any direction. For this one, I have the ears facing full to the side. Draw a "center" line down the back of the ear. Round off from the front of the ear where the folds are drawn in to the back centerline. Hollow out the inside of the ear. Hollow out a bit behind the flare of the ear on both sides.

Carve the nostril using your No. 2 blade, being careful to hold it perpendicular to the nostril line, and incise straight downward around only the back half. Then use your ⅛-inch gouge to hollow out the nostril hole, starting shallow at the front, going deeper toward the back, stopping at the line you incised. After you have done this, carve the fold of skin (the tail of the "6"). Incise perpendicular to the line; then carve out the side on the top. After the hole is the depth you wish, bevel the edges of the nostril hole slightly. Only after you have beveled the edges, deepen the hole and undermine the back portion slightly. Hollow out slightly around the outside edge of the nostril hole with your gouge. Hollow out the deepest between the upper lip and the nostril hole, and only very slightly around the back of the nostril hole.

To prepare for carving the mouth, draw in the lines of the tongue, the teeth, and the lips. Carve in layers, the innermost—the tongue—first. Using the edge of your No. 22 blade, press it in and roll it along the side from one side around to the other. Use the small V tool to carve out the tongue. Round over with the No. 22 blade. Carve out the bottom and top teeth using the same procedure. Bevel the upper and lower lips slightly, and hollow out the inside top of the mouth with the ⅛-inch gouge. Make small V cuts to demarcate the teeth. A mature horse has 6 teeth (incisors) that show on the top, and 6 on the bottom. Then there is a gap, which is where the bit fits, and then the molars, which do not show.

For carving the eye, use your No. 2 blade. Be careful to remain perpendicular to the line you have drawn for the eye; incise along the line. Make a dot, just off center of the middle of the eyeball. Round off from this point to the line you cut, to form the eyeball. Be sure to carve the edges deep enough or the eyeball will look flat.

Incise along the brow line drawn from the back corner of the eye, then carve down the lower edge of the eyelid to the corner. Do not round the lower edge over to the eyeball until you have carved the eyelid. After you have carved the eyelid, round over the back ⅔ of the lower lid to the eyeball. Hollow out the front ⅓ below the eyelid. Round over the

top eyelid to the eyeball all the way, including the fold from the back corner of the eye. Use the small V tool to cut a shallow, short, inverted arched line just under the eyeball to the lower eyelid. Do the same over the entire top of the eye and rear eye fold to form the upper eyelid. Bevel both of the cuts out on the side next to the eyeball.

Carve out the details on the headstall and any other decorations. Carve out the mane hair flow as you did the hair flow for the tail and sand out (4-46).

Carving the Body

Step 17. To prepare for carving the body, first trace around the legs and the head you have carved at their attachment points. Turn the neck slightly to add the impression of movement. Move the legs in approximately ³⁄₁₆ inch (½ cm). Do not draw in the details of the saddle and other decorations yet or they will become skewed from the rounding off/roughing out process (4-47).

Using your angle grinder with the coarse sanding attachment, or the large cylinder burr on your rotary tool, or 1-inch gouge and mallet, round over the top and bottom shaping around the leg and neck attachments (4-48, 4-49, 4-50).

4-47 As you rough out the body and round it off, the details of the saddle and other decoration are not yet drawn, as seen in side view.

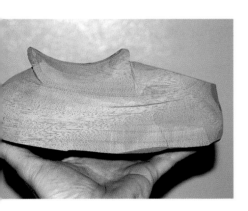

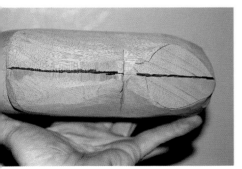

4-48 A centerline is maintained and the area where the neck attaches is shaped to match the head and neck piece, as seen in top view.

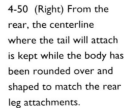

4-49 (Left) From the front, the body has been rounded over and shaped to match the front leg and neck attachments.

4-50 (Right) From the rear, the centerline where the tail will attach is kept while the body has been rounded over and shaped to match the rear leg attachments.

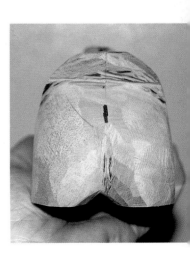

Assembling the Animal & Finishing

Step 18. After the body is roughed out, glue the head and legs into position. Drill a hole for the tail and check for fit, but do not glue it into position yet (4-51). Take note that you can use a PVA wood glue to glue the legs and neck into position only if you have mirror-smooth, perfectly flush surfaces. If not, use a thick epoxy resin glue.

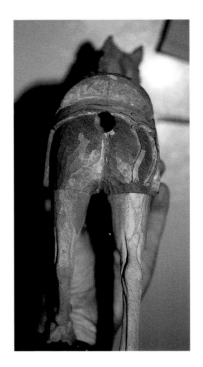

4-51 The head and legs have been glued into position and a hole has been drilled for the tail.

4-52 The saddle and other decorations are drawn on the left side, or inside relative to the position on the carousel.

4-53 The saddle and other decorations are drawn on the right side, or Romance side.

Adding the Saddle & Other Decorations

Step 19. Draw your saddle and other decorations on both sides (4-52). Remember, with very few exceptions, on American figures, the right side, or Romance side, is much more decorated (4-53). You can trace the saddle, etc., from the pattern onto the wood, following the curve, or draw it freehand.

The breast strap on a carousel horse generally follows the line where the head/neck is joined to the torso, which helps to disguise the line where the two parts join. That is the case with this figure, so before drawing in the chest strap, shape in the two parts by carving and sanding. The top edge of the strap will follow this line.

Step 20. Start carving out the saddle and other decorations. Working in layers, you will carve away some of the lines you have drawn in. Just draw them back when you have carved down to the desired level.

Carve out first the areas with the deepest layers around the straps, the edges of the outermost blankets, etc. Round out the chest, belly, and curve of the shoulder while you are doing this. You will want to leave the tail out so that you can properly shape the buttocks.

Carve out the next layer: the rump strap, chest strap, and curls at the bottom of the blanket (4-54, 4-55). Bevel down to the top of the rings holding the ribbons. Carve out around the top of the ribbons. After you have done this, round out the top of the ribbons and carve a wavy flow into the ribbons.

Carve the next layer: the rear blanket (4-56, 4-57). Round off the back edge. Don't just make the blanket flat; carve some flow into it as if it is billowing in the wind from the motion of the horse.

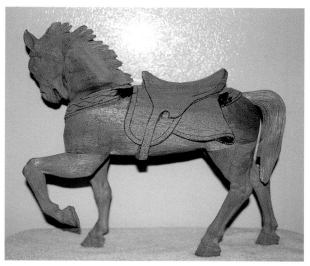

4-54 On the left side, the shaded areas indicate where to carve to define the rump strap, chest strap, and curls at the bottom of the blanket.

4-56 On the right side, the shaded areas indicate where to carve to define the rear blanket.

4-55 On the right side, the shaded areas indicate where to carve to define the rump strap, chest strap, and curls at the bottom of the blanket.

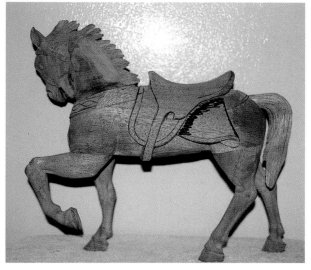

4-57 On the left side, the shaded areas indicate where to carve to define the rear blanket.

Carve out the next layer: around the saddle and girth strap (4-58, 4-59).

Carve out the girth belt buckle and round over the girth strap (4-60, 4-61). Refine the shape of the saddle. Undercut the lower edge of the blanket and girth strap and other appropriate areas. Carve out the flowers (4-62).

Sanding & Final Detailing

Step 21. Smooth the carving by sanding out using 80-grit sandpaper and then carve in the flow lines, fringe, and other details on the decorations. Use a wood-burning pen to burn in lines for fringe, as shown in 4-63.

4-58 On the left side, the shaded areas indicate where to carve to define the saddle and girth strap.

4-60 On the right side, now you can carve out the girth belt buckle and round over the girth strap.

4-59 On the right side, the shaded areas indicate where to carve to define the saddle and girth strap.

4-61 On the left side, now you can round over the girth strap.

4-62 The flowers are carved out.

On Carving Your Miniature Carousel Horse

I hope I have succeeded in guiding you through the making of a small carousel horse and that it is something of which you are proud, a family heirloom. Is it everything you had hoped for? I hope not. If it is, then I've failed. I've been carving carousel horses for over ten years now and have yet to be completely satisfied with one. There is always room for improvement.

Guess what? If you are now ready to tackle a full-size figure, it's because you have already been through all the necessary steps. The only difference is the amount of wood you use, and when you laminate the wood for the body, leave it hollow in the center. You will also want to use power tools to a greater extent to remove the bulk of the wood in the rough stages of the carving.

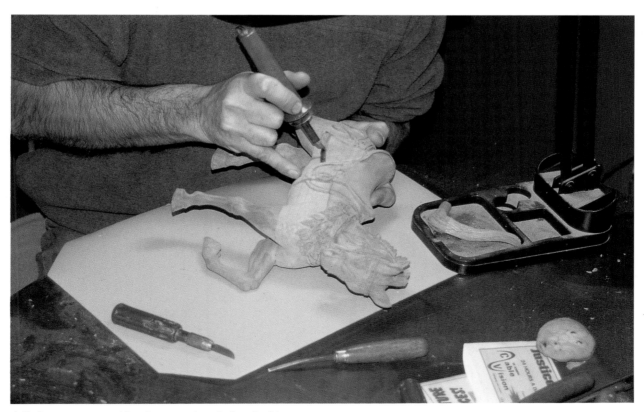

4-63 Bruce uses a wood-burning pen to burn in lines for fringe.

Draw in the musculature for the shoulders, thighs, and flank (4-64, 4-65). Then carve out and sand, sanding out entire figure with 120-grit sandpaper.

Finishing

Step 22. If you are going to leave your figure with a natural finish, seal with a clear wood finish (4-66).

4-64 On the left side, the shaded areas indicate where to carve to define the musculature for the shoulders, thighs, and flank.

4-65 On the right side, the shaded areas indicate where to carve to define the musculature for the shoulders, thighs, and flank.

Buff out with 220-grit sandpaper, using a light touch. Repeat this procedure at least three times. Softer, more open-grained wood will require this step as many as seven times.

If you intend to paint your figure, spray on an inexpensive, flat white spray paint. You will be amazed at how many scratches, nicks and other flaws this will disclose, which are not evident with a natural finish. Sand out or otherwise correct these defects. Sand and seal, sand and seal, using the white paint, the same as in doing a natural finish figure, and then paint as you desire.

Finish with a spray of clear coat. If you try to brush on the clear coat over a painted surface, the colors are prone to bleed into each other. The same applies if you do more than spray a very light coat for the first coat. Spray on the clear coat in two or three applications.

4-66 Finished miniature parade horse designed by Solomon Stein and Harry Goldstein, circa 1912. The horse, carved from Honduran mahogany, is finished with a clear gloss.

ᴀ Carving Your Own Carousel Animal Full Size

A full-size carousel animal can seem an overwhelming project, even more so than a miniature tabletop model. It can also become quite expensive, as a great deal of wood is required and you may not have all the tools to do a full-size figure in the conventional or traditional way. I will show you ways around all of these obstacles.

Almost Like Carving in Miniature— Just a Matter of Scale

So, take a deep breath and let's get started. Carving the full-size figure is a matter of proceeding through a series of stages, just as for the miniature carving—you may find it not so overwhelming after all (5-1).

5-1 (FACING PAGE) The painted and natural finished full-size Stein & Goldstein parade horse, from Pattern 8, carved in this chapter is shown with the miniature figure carved in Chapter 4.

First of all, wood can be quite expensive, but it doesn't have to be. The figure I'm doing is the same one I used for the miniature, the parade horse stander, Pattern 8, designed by Solomon Stein and Harry Goldstein, circa 1912. It is one of the largest carousel figures ever made. The wood for it cost me less than $200. You can make an average-size carousel figure for about half that—but not if you use basswood (*Tilia* spp.), Honduran mahogany (*Swietenia macrophylla*), or other woods typically used by carvers; they would cost about five times as much.

So how do I cut my costs so dramatically? I use construction-grade lumber. But you have to be careful and know what to look for.

Once you get your wood to your shop, stack it with spacers between each row and let it rest for at least a week to stabilize it in your shop's heat and humidity. This is especially important if the lumber was exposed to the weather. If the lumber was housed indoors in a climate-controlled facility, a day or two will suffice. If you don't allow the wood to adjust to your shop, you may be in for a rude surprise. Nothing is more heartbreaking than to be proudly showing your newly finished carousel figure, when you hear a loud "snap!" and a crack appears before your (and your friends') eyes.

❧ On Selecting Wood

Most construction-grade lumber comes in standard lengths and widths, is kiln dried, and has already been surfaced and edged, eliminating the need for a planer and joiner. But be aware that a nominal "2 x 4" is actually 1½ inches by 3½ inches; a "2 x 6" is actually 1½ inches by 5½ inches, etc. This is precisely because they have been surfaced and edged. However, for convenience's sake, I will use here the generic terms 2 x 4, 2 x 6, etc. And be careful where you buy your wood. True, construction-grade lumber may be kiln dried, but that doesn't really mean much if the lumber is left exposed to the weather.

Most construction-grade lumber will be marked "P.S.F." This means "pine, spruce, fir." What you are getting will be one of these. It won't do you any good to ask the store which it is; they won't know. So it gets a little tricky. You can use any of the three, but not all wood is created equal. In most of the United States, 2 x 4s and 2 x 6s are generally spruce (*Picea sitchensis*), which carves very well. I actually prefer it to basswood (*Tilia* spp.). The 2 x 8s, 2 x 10s and 2 x 12s will generally be either ponderosa pine (*Pinus ponderosa*) or fir (*Pseudotsuga menziesii*). Ponderosa pine carves pretty well if you keep your tools sharp. Fir is the worst of the three; it has a tendency to "crush" or "shred," but if you keep your tools very sharp or use rotary tools for the detail work, you will be okay. If you live on the American West Coast, you are likely to get fir or western cedar (*Thuja plicata*). Western cedar works about like fir, but be careful. It smells great, but is actually mildly toxic. If you don't use proper respirators, you will end up with headaches and perhaps some mild respiratory distress.

If you live in the American South, you may have a problem. The wood available is longleaf pine (*Pinus palustris*) or slash pine (*Pinus elliottii*). You can tell because the grain will be very bold and distinct. Herein lies the problem. While the grain is especially interesting and beautiful, the dark grain (summer wood) is very hard, while the light grain (spring wood) is very soft. It's the contrast that causes problems. You had best resign yourself to using all power tools.

If you live in Canada or Europe, you have hit the jackpot. The construction-grade lumber available in these regions, in all widths, is generally spruce (*Picea sitchensis*).

In Australia, most of the construction-grade lumber will be lauan (*Shorea* spp.) from the Philippines or Indonesia, or jarrah, a native eucalyptus (*Eucalyptus marginata*). They all carve pretty well. If you are lucky, you may get tanguile, which is wonderful to carve; very unlucky and you will get Australian pine (*Casuarina* spp.), also known as "ironwood."

Most of you will be dealing with ponderosa pine, spruce or fir. How do you tell them apart?

Spruce (*Picea sitchensis*) is the lightest in color. It is a clear white with light, indistinct grain. It has a moderate, resinous, clean "Pine Sol" smell to it. When you cut with the grain, it will "sing" to you in a clear "high C." It is the preferred wood for fine musical instruments for its resonant qualities.

Ponderosa pine (*Pinus ponderosa*) is only slightly darker than spruce and has a similar smell, but not as strong. The main tip-off is that it is not nearly as musical when being cut.

Fir (*Pseudotsuga menziesii*) will be just slightly darker than ponderosa pine. It has a less strong odor than spruce or pine, and the grain is more distinct.

Since all of these woods can have a lot of knots, which you want to avoid as much as possible, you will need to sort through the stock at the lumber store personally, which may annoy the sales staff. But if you tell them what you are using it for, they will often give you enthusiastic help instead.

Enlarging the Plan & Making Templates

Make your pattern from your original sketch or blueprint. A full-size carousel figure is generally larger than you can enlarge on a standard copy machine. Sometimes your friendly neighborhood architectural firm will let you use their blueprint copy machine, but if you are like most of us, you will have to do it the old fashioned way—by graphing. I generally use poster board for my full-size patterns.

Draw a graph over your original sketch or blueprint using one-inch squares. Depending on how large your full-size figure will be, determine mathematically how large you need to make your squares for your full-size grid. For your typical full-size figure, your grid squares will need to be 4 to 6 inches. Using your grid, plot and draw from the original sketch to your full-size grid to make your pattern.

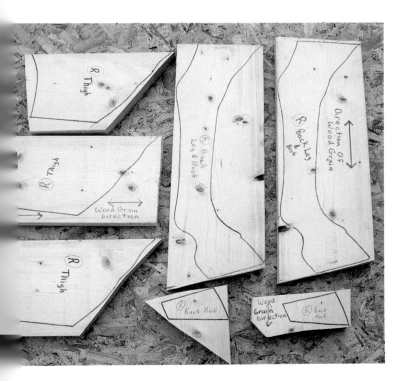

5-2 Cut the sections apart on the boards.

✎ Cutting Out the Parts

Cut the parts apart on the board using a saws-all or jigsaw, but do not try to cut each part out with anything but a band saw or you will get a skewed cut (see slides of parts cut apart, and slide of parts cut out before and after glue-up). It is very important to spread the glue evenly on each section. If you are unsure of how much glue or how many clamps to use, err on the side of caution. Use too much glue and too many clamps rather than not enough. Screw the clamps down as tightly as you can. If the clamps crush into the wood, it can be fixed later.

Laminating the Carving Blocks & Assembling

Cut your pattern into the component parts of a carousel figure, as described for a miniature figure. Draw your pattern on the wood as described for a miniature figure. I generally use nominal 2-inch stock. For a full-size figure, especially if people will ride it, it is very important to pay attention to the direction of the wood grain and to cut the parts out appropriately for maximum strength (as outlined for a miniature figure). The numbers I use are for a typical full-size figure of 4½- to 5-feet long. I am making a larger figure to illustrate this project, but all the principles are the same.

Back Legs

For the back legs cut the pattern in half at the knee. Cut out three sections for the thigh with the grain running horizontal (5-2). Cut two sections out for the leg and hooves with the wood grain running vertical. Cut out one more section for the hoof only. Split this section in half. Glue up the thigh and leg-hoof sections using 6-inch "C" clamps (5-3).

Front Legs

If you are making a "stander," one leg will generally be straight, one bent. For "jumpers," both legs will be bent. For a straight leg, cut two parts out, running the wood grain vertically from the hoof to the forearm. Cut a third section out, grain running vertically, for the forearm (knee to where forearm meets torso). Cut a third section out for the hoof and split it in half as you did for the back leg. For a bent front leg, cut three sections out for the forearm and two for the canon and hoof. Cut a third section out for the hoof and split it in half. Glue the sections up as described for the back legs (5-4).

Be sure to glue the third section for the thigh (back legs) and arm (front legs) on the inside of that part. There is a right and a left.

When laminated, the hooves (front and back) should be approximately 4½- to 5-inches thick (5-5). Pastern to knee, approximately 3-inches thick. Thigh and arms approximately 4½ to 5 inches.

5-3 Using "C" clamps to laminate the cut-out sections together for the back leg.

5-4 Using "C" clamps to laminate the cut-out sections together for the front leg.

5-5 The straight front leg.

Joining the Leg Pieces

For the front leg the arm is joined to the canon, and for the back leg, the thigh to the leg.

Ensure that the parts to be joined are mirror smooth. You will need a large, stationary disk sander to accomplish this. If you do not have access to this piece of equipment, bear with me, and I will outline an alternative for you.

You will need large (3- to 4-inch) deck screws, two for each joint. First, with the two parts held together (no glue yet!), drill a pilot hole for the screws, from each side of the leg (front and back) at an angle from one part into the other part (5-6). You will need a 6-inch drill bit for this. You may want to clamp the parts down to your workbench to hold them in place while drilling these pilot holes. Remember that you have a right and a left leg, and position the parts accordingly with the third laminated section of the arm or thigh positioned so it will be on the inside (belly or chest) when the finished part is attached to the torso of your figure.

Use a ½-inch or ⅝-inch drill bit to countersink the screws. Drill the countersink hole following the route drilled by your pilot hole to an appropriate depth so that when you screw in your screws, they will get a good grip on both parts. Spread glue evenly on one side or the other of the parts to be joined. Sink the screws in tightly until you can see glue being squeezed out around the glue joint.

If you use brass or zinc-coated screws, you can fill in over the screw heads and you are done joining your two parts together. But if this is going to be a working carousel figure, subject to the elements, after the glue has dried, back the screws out. Finish drilling, along the course of your pilot

✒ *Joining Parts*

If you do not have access to a large, stationary disk grinder that you can use to get a mirror-smooth surface, use automotive putty (Bondo or other product) to achieve a tight joint.

Use a ½-inch or ⅝-inch drill bit to drill 2 to 4 holes approximately 1-inch deep on each surface to be joined, at eccentric angles. Drill pilot holes and countersink holes as previously described.

Using refrigerated, pure putty (not mixed with sawdust), mix the putty and spread on both surfaces to be joined, ensuring that the putty is pressed into the previously drilled holes. Remember your latex gloves. Put the screws in as previously described. Work quickly! If the putty sets before you have the screws securely in place, you will have to grind or carve the putty off, redrill all your holes, and start again.

For a working figure, after the putty has set, back the screws out and dowel as previously described.

hole, using the same size drill bit as you did for your countersink hole. Pound wood dowel rods, coated with glue, completely into the holes. Cut off flush with the part..

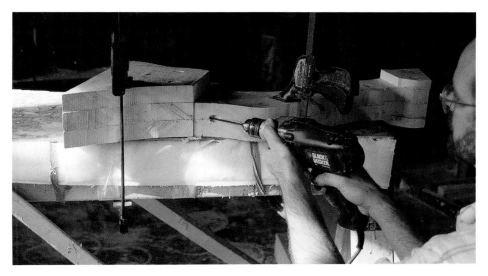

5-6 Drilling pilot holes to join the leg and the thigh. It is very important that parts be exactly flush before drilling these pilot holes.

Shaping the Legs

You are now ready to start shaping the legs. Draw in the front and back profiles as described for a small figure. In carving this time though, you will want to use a saws-all to cut away excess wood (5-7). An angle grinder with a donut-shaped carbide grinding wheel is useful for rough shaping (5-8). The angle grinder with a flat grinding disk can be used to refine the shape (5-9).

Laminating the Body

One of the most common questions I get is, "Where do you find a piece of wood big enough to carve such a large figure?" The answer is, I don't. I glue up the torso of the carousel figure in such a way that it is largely hollow. Basically, I'm making a hollow box in the shape of a horse's body (5-10).

There are several reasons for this. One is that it uses far less wood and is thus less expensive. Another is that it makes the figure considerably lighter, which is a concern for an operating carousel. But the main reason is that by laminating the wood properly, it can be made much stronger. It is also much less likely to crack as the figure ages. As wood ages, it shrinks slightly, even if it is properly kiln dried when new. The thicker the wood, the more apparent the shrinkage will be, in the form of cracks on the exterior. A hollow figure is proportionately less thick and will thus shrink (crack) proportionately less.

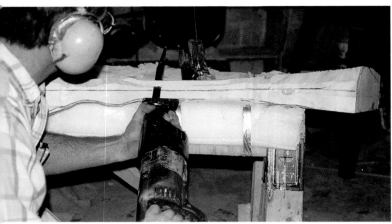

5-7 Using a saws-all to cut the excess wood away for the front and back profiles.

5-8 Using the angle grinder with the donut-shaped carbide grinding wheel to rough shape the leg.

5-9 Using the angle grinder with the coarse, flat grinding disc to refine your roughed-out shape.

5-10 The torso is hollow, assembled from laminated pieces.

❧ *Making a Hollow Torso*

This is how it's done. You first need to laminate the left and right side panels for the torso. I use 2 x 4 boards for this. Cut the boards to the appropriate length as indicated by your pattern. For a typical carousel figure, this will be 3- to 4-feet long. You will probably need 12 to 15 boards cut to the proper length for each side.

Glue and clamp the appropriate number of boards together, 4-inch side to 4-inch side. Be sure to use plenty of glue and spread the glue evenly on the side facing out on each successive board, except for the last board to be laminated, which does not need any glue.

Clamp the boards tightly together using bar clamps. You need 6 bar clamps to do this properly. Torque the clamps as tightly as you can. Glue should be squeezed out on both sides. Let the glue set up for at least 6 hours before removing the clamps; 24 hours before moving on to the next step.

Cut out the belly and back sections for the torso. You will need 2 x 6 boards for this. You want the body to be approximately 12-inches thick for a typical, full-size figure. Since the side panels are each 3½-inches thick for a total of 7 inches, cut 6 of these boards (3 for the belly and 3 for the back) to the same length as you did the boards for the side panels. Trace the top 5½ inches from the top of your pattern (back) on 3 of these boards and the bottom 5½ inches (belly) from your pattern on 3 of these boards. Draw a straight line from front to back on your pattern to represent the top and bottom (belly and back) 6 inches. Cut the belly and back sections out on your band saw.

Cut out the chest and butt sections for the torso. Again, use 2 x 6 boards. Measure in 5½ inches from the front (chest) and back (butt) on your pattern. Sketch a straight line between your previously drawn "back" 5½ inches and "belly" 5½ inches. Cut these two sections out (butt and chest) from your torso pattern. Use these to trace on your wood 3 "butt" sections and 3 "chest" sections. Cut these sections out with your band saw running the grain of the wood vertically.

After you have cut out the wood sections of the belly, back, butt and chest on your band saw, tape your pattern back together. Using your pattern, trace the torso onto your previously laminated side panels. Cut out your side panels preferably using your band saw, if you can physically handle it. But for a full-size figure, these side panels will likely be too heavy and bulky for you to manipulate through your band saw. If so, cut the side panels out using your saws-all. Take care to keep your saws-all blade perpendicular to your cut, or you will get a skewed cut, ruining your side panel.

Putting the Pieces Together

You are now ready to laminate the torso together. First put together the inside frames for the torso. Each frame consists of one back section, one belly section, one chest section, and one butt section (refer to 5-10). Find a flat surface and line the sections up in their proper positions on top of your pattern. Spread glue on the edges that meet.

Using large wood screws, draw the section up tight, until the glue is being squeezed out. Put together the appropriate number of frames, which when laminated to the two side panels, will give you the appropriate thickness for the torso of your carousel figure.

Stack up your side panels and inside frames, spreading glue copiously between each section. Many turn-of-the-century and contemporary carvers put notes, current newspaper articles, or mementos inside before joining the last side panel, making the carousel figure a time capsule.

Clamp the laminated sections tightly together using bar clamps (5-11). Be sure to use at least 8 clamps. More is better. Remove all the screws that were in the frames.

5-11 Use bar clamps to laminate the torso.

The Head & Neck Section

The head on the average size carousel horse should be laminated as a solid block as described in the sidebar to the right. For a large figure with a large head, such as a lion or an elephant, you may want to make it hollow (5-12), using the technique described in the sidebar on making a hollow torso that is on page 125.

So depending on your figure, go ahead and laminate the neck and head section either solid or so they will be hollow. If holow, laminate up to approximately 8 inches, running the grain vertically (shoulder to head).

Now join the head to the neck (5-13). Note that if the head is tucked tightly, as is commonly the case in John Zalar and Stein & Goldstein figures, you need to carve the head and neck before joining them. This is how I am doing it (5-14). The area where the neck and head join together must be perfectly flat and level for a good strong fit. However, unless you have a large, industrial disk grinder, this is virtually impossible. To get around this problem, I usually join the body sections together with automotive putty. When the parts are squeezed together, the putty will level them out.

Use a 1-inch drill bit to sink holes at eccentric angles at least one inch deep on both the head and neck where they will join together. Add a couple in the center of each piece (unless the parts are laminated hollow), then 4 to 6 around these two.

5-13 An example of the head block attached to the neck. This is from the making of "Betty's Muller Ghost Horse," a design inspired by the Muller brothers that Bruce is making on commission.

5-12 For a large figure, the neck is also hollow.

5-14 The head block is being carved separately for this large stander, Pattern 8, designed by Solomon Stein and Harry Goldstein.

5-15 The head and neck joined together, showing how the strap conceals the joint.

Use refrigerated, pure (not mixed with sawdust) automotive putty, such as Bondo. You must work very quickly. Activate the Bondo and spread on both surfaces. Fill the pre-drilled holes completely and spread approximately ¼ inch thick on both sides. Press together tightly and hold in position until the Bondo sets up. You may want to pre-drill some holes on each side, front and back, and screw the two parts together and hold them together until the Bondo sets. But don't forget to take the screws out! You may also want to cock the head by pivoting it slightly off a straight axis on the neck; this adds life and animation to your figure. Consider getting someone to help you with this step—if the Bondo sets up before you finish, you will have to grind all the Bondo off and redrill your holes.

The placement of the neck strap on this figure is not arbitrary. It conceals the seam line where the two parts meet (5-15).

Making the Tail

You will need to laminate the tail at least 2 boards thick (approximately 3 to 4 inches). This gives you enough thickness to allow for a good "wavy" flow. This is important, as the attitude of the tail imparts a good portion of the animation and excitement to the figure. This is why I don't like to use real horsehair tails. They just hang there. No illusion of motion at all—likewise, if you carve a wood tail hanging straight down in one plane.

5-16 The parts of the tail are cut out and laminated together.

Unless the tail is streaming out behind the horse, you need to make the tail in two sections to ensure strength. Run the grain as shown in 5-16. After the glue has set up for the laminated sections, use a large stationary sanding disk to make the surfaces to be joined mirror smooth. Use large wood screws to draw the parts together tightly, sinking them through pre-drilled holes and countersink holes. After the glue has set up at least 6 hours, back the screws out and replace with ½-inch dowel rods.

Shape and carve as outlined for small figures, doing the bulk wood removal and rough shaping with your saws-all and wood-grinding wheel. Put the hair flow in using the edge of the coarse-grit sanding disk on your angle grinder. You can actually get a more natural flow using these methods than if you carve them by hand. I actually do the entire tail with my saws-all, grinding wheel, and grinding disk, finishing it up with hand sanding, using a folded, 40-grit piece of sandpaper.

Assembling the Main Parts of Your Carousel Figure

Follow the same steps as described in joining the head and the neck to join the head/neck and the legs to the torso (5-17, 5-18, 5-19). As with a miniature figure, you will need to fine tune where these parts meet, using your grinder, carving tools and sandpaper. As with the point where the head and neck join, the placement of the chest strap is no accident. You can use it to cover the seam line where the neck meets the torso. Likewise, you may want to devise some kind of strap, ribbons, flowers, etc., to cover up or draw attention away from where the legs meet the torso. This is another advantage of sculpting decorations on with putty rather than carving them directly from the wood.

Attaching the Tail

The tail needs to be anchored very firmly as children love to climb on and hang from it (5-20). This is also another reason: it is better to use a wood tail rather than a real horsehair tail on a working carousel figure. A real horsehair tail loses its hair at an alarming rate.

You should have a section at least 4-inches long and 2-inches in diameter, which extends from the top of the tail. Using a 2-inch hole saw, drill into the hollow space inside the torso at the point where you want to place the tail. Push this section of the tail firmly into the hole. If it does not fit snugly, fill in any spaces with putty. Use two, ½-inch dowel rods going from above the tail, piercing through the tail. If the tail is long enough and one of the back legs is angled back, you can further secure the tail by doweling it to the inside of the back leg.

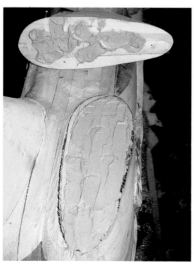

5-17 and 5-18 Anchor holes are drilled on both surfaces at eccentric angles. Then pure automotive putty is generously applied on both surfaces.

5-19 Joining the body parts together using putty and dowel rods.

5-20 The body parts are carved out and joined together, including the tail.

Carving & Sculpting Techniques

The parts are laminated together and rough shaped, having followed the same steps as for a small figure, but having used primarily an angle grinder for bulk wood removal. Now comes the detail carving. Here you must decide whether to carve the details out of the wood or to sculpt them on with a putty, such as Bondo. I nearly always

sculpt on the bridle and any other decorations using the automotive putty; it is much easier to get the face of the figure, the most critical part of your carving, correct, without having to work around the decorations. This is the method I will show you with examples from this Stein & Goldstein horse project and from another project called "Paul's horse." However, if you choose to do your figure completely from wood, be sure to carve the face a little fatter than it should be to allow you to carve the bridle and other details out of the wood.

Carving the Halter

After the face is completely carved, sketch in the bridle and other decorations on the wood (see 5-14). Drill ¼- to ½-inch holes, approximately ½-inch deep, at eccentric angles at spaced intervals inside your sketched outline (5-21). These are the anchor holes for your bridle, etc., on the wood.

Use refrigerated automotive putty, such as Bondo, thickened with sawdust. Doing only a small area at a time, press the putty mix into the anchor holes and sculpt on the bridle, etc., using your fingers (5-22). Remember to use latex gloves and to keep your fingers wet. Work quickly and don't try to be exact. This step is rough modeling only.

Re-sketch/define your design on the putty-sculpted bridle, etc. (5-23). Using your wood carving tools, fine-tune your design (5-24).

Carving a Rosebud

Lay out a design on the wood (5-25). Mold an automotive putty and sawdust paste to approximate the shape of the flower (5-26). Redraw the rose on the set-up putty mix (5-27).

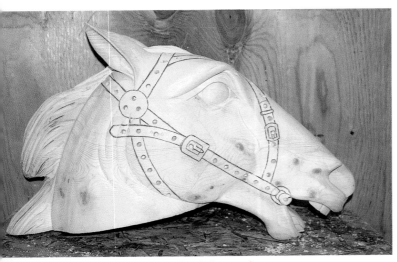

5-21 Drill your anchor holes.

5-22 Rough sculpt on your putty/sawdust mixture.

5-23 Define your edges.

5-24 Carve out the buckles.

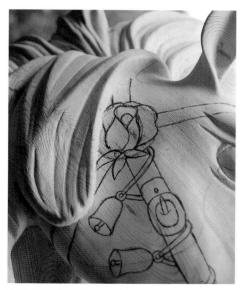

5-25 First draw in your design.

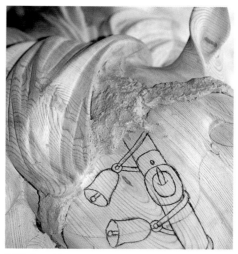

5-26 Roughly model on refrigerated Bondo/sawdust mixture. You must work quickly and don't try to do too large an area at a time.

5-27 Sketch your design back onto the carving.

Carve out outline of rosebud (5-28). Carve out and shape the petioles (leaves). Incise along the lines drawn for the rosebud. This way, as you carve the layers, your lines will still be there. Start from the outside and work in. Carve out the outer petals first. Be sure to think three dimensionally; i.e., be sure to recurve the petals, include undulations, etc., just like a real petal. It might be helpful to go to a florist and get a real rosebud to use as a model. I commonly use the flowers pictured on sympathy cards for my models. Round over the central bud.

Use your ¼-inch gouge to hollow out just inside the lip of the bud.

Carve out the inside of the bud. Do your undercuts on the petals. This adds a great deal of depth. I undercut these petals only very slightly as this figure will be used to make a mold to manufacture plastic replicas.

Use fine sandpaper to sand smooth and gypsum wallboard putty to fill in any small voids left from bubbles when mixing the Bondo mixture (5-29). Let dry, then sand smooth (5-30).

5-28 Carve from the outside in. First incise straight down along all of your lines so you don't lose them as you carve the different levels.

5-29 Using 120-grit, closed coat sandpaper (cut from a belt sanding belt), sand, and then fill in any flaws (pinholes, etc.), using wallboard putty.

5-30 A finished rose bud, ready to paint.

5-31 and 5-32 Cutting the rough outline for diamonds and pearls and then their finished shape.

Carving Diamonds & Pearls

These examples come from a project called "Paul's horse." Lay out the design on the wood. Model Bondo and sawdust paste into the rough shape of diamonds and pearls. Since these are small, it may be easier for you to just lay down a flat strip approximately ½-inch thick.

Refine the outline of the diamonds and pearls using your craft knife or sharp pocketknife. If you laid down a flat strip, draw in diamonds and pearls, then cut out shapes with your craft knife or sharp pocketknife (5-31). Make stop cuts where diamonds and pearls meet. Draw a line from point to point across the widest point of your diamonds. Cut down from your line to your stop cuts.

Finish cutting out the circle for your pearls. Carve down the top of the pearl to just above where you carved down to your stop cut between the diamonds and pearls. Round over your pearls. Draw a line down the center of your diamonds from end to end.

Bevel off the four edges of your diamonds from near the bottom edges to your centerline. Fill in imperfections with gypsum wallboard putty, then using 120-grit sandpaper, sand smooth (5-32).

Carving a Bell

Lay out design on wood. Drill hole to anchor the Bondo and sawdust paste. Model catalyzed Bondo and sawdust paste into rough shape of bell (5-33). Using a craft knife or sharp pocketknife, define shape of bell.

Draw in, then carve out, the clapper and inside of bell. First incise straight line as stop cut along the side of the clapper. Then using ¼-gauge palm chisel, hollow out the inside of the bell to your stop cuts. Define the shape of the clapper (5-34). Incise a line straight down between the ring at the top of the bell and the body of the bell, as a stop cut. Incise down approximately ½ thickness of the bell. Carve out the bell ring to the stop cut.

Round over the top of the bell. Round over the sides of the bell. You will need to hollow out slightly along the lip of the bell. Drill out the center of the bell. Sculpt the string suspending the bell from the chest strap. One side goes over the top of the ring; the other comes from under the ring. Fill in any imperfections and sand smooth with 120-grit sandpaper.

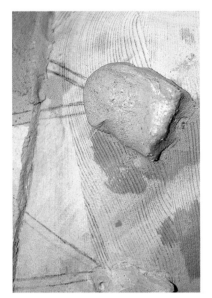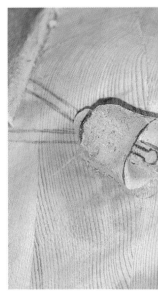

5-33 and 5-34 Applying the rough shape of the bell and then carving the details.

Finishing & Painting Techniques

Now that your carousel figure is carved and assembled, you must decide how to finish it. Do you prefer a natural finish showing the wood grain or a fully painted one? I'll demonstrate both with a step-by-step guide. I'll use a natural finish on the Stein & Goldstein parade horse you have seen replicated in this chapter. My daughter Charity will demonstrate painting technique on the original Applebee horse carving, which needed refinishing, having recently been the model for a new mold.

Natural Finish

For the Stein & Goldstein carousel horse, I used construction grade lumber, which has a light shade, giving me some leeway in the finished color.

Step 1. Before you assemble the figure, all of the parts should be carved and at least rough sanded. Once the figure is assembled, hand sand the entire figure with medium-grit (80-grit) and then fine-grit (120-grit) sandpaper (5-35). Do not try to use any power sanding tools at this point. You will only end up with flat spots where it should be rounded. Like it or not, there is no substitute for hand sanding. I advise that you purchase some rubber fingertip protectors at your local office supply store...unless you like raw fingertips.

✺ When Not to Seal

When a figure is going to be painted, I use a sanding sealer between sandings, but do NOT use sanding sealer at this point if you intend to do a natural finish. There are wood preparations on the market that claim they enable you to stain wood evenly, but that would defeat your purpose here. If you use them, you may as well just paint your figure.

The whole point of using stain is to enhance the wood grain, not hide it. Indentations and hollows will absorb more stain, making them darker, high points less, making them lighter, thus more nearly mimicking the shadows and highlights of a real animal.

Also, on this figure, we are going to bleach the wood on the mane, tail, a blaze on the face, and socks on the legs. If you seal the wood, you cannot do this.

5-35 The decorations for the parade horse stander designed by Solomon Stein and Harry Goldstein have been completed and the figure is sanded and ready for painting.

Yᴏᴜ can buy wood bleach at most full-service hardware/lumber stores. Be sure you read and understand the instructions fully. This is potent stuff; it can cause serious burns. If it splashes on your clothes, it will bleach them pure white…or even burn holes in them. Follow instructions for application carefully. One application to the desired area will suffice for pine, spruce, or fir. For darker woods, you will need additional applications. You can even bleach black walnut white with 3 to 4 applications.

Step 2. Bleach out the parts you want to stay lighter colored. If you don't, even spruce will turn a light amber, pine and fir a butterscotch color, when you apply your clear coat.

Step 3. Paint the areas you want painted, the bridle, saddle, blankets, flowers, etc. I prefer to use acrylic paints. They have a latex (rubber) base and can thus "breathe" with the wood. For this figure, I am going to "crack" the paint to give it an antique appearance. First, apply a dark base paint, usually dark brown or black, to the areas you want to paint (5-36).

Step 4. Apply stain to the areas you want stained. I prefer to use the thin, brush-on stain such as Min Wax rather than paste stains. Remember, the stain will soak into the wood and bleed into it beyond where you are staining approximately ¼ to ½ inch, so allow for this when applying. If you get stain where you don't want it, you must either learn to live with it or carve it off, which could disfigure your carving, especially a small figure.

Step 5. Seal the wood now, after you have bleached and stained your figure. Especially if you have bleached sections as I have with this figure, you may want to use a spray sealer. I prefer to use Deft, which is a form of lacquer, but any clear wood finish will do. Be advised that polyurethane and some other finishes, though advertised as

5-36 A black base paint has been applied to all areas that are to be painted because we are going to crackle the paint.

✑ Applying Stain

Wʜen you apply the stain, any scratches or other blemishes in the wood will absorb more stain, which will highlight them. So ensure that all scratches and blemishes are sanded out before applying the stain, unless you want to highlight the imperfections.

"clear," do have a light amber color, and your bleached wood will take on that color. So try to use water clear finish to avoid tinting.

Likewise, just because you are using water clear finish on your wood, don't assume you can skip the bleaching step for areas you want to remain white. If you don't bleach before applying any clear finish, terpenes (a chemical in plants) in the wood will oxidize, turning the wood darker, even with a water clear finish. Using bleach burns out the terpenes and pigments so that the wood remains white after applying the clear sealer.

Step 6. After spraying on a light coat of clear wood sealer, lightly sand the entire figure with fine sandpaper. Seal again and sand again. For pine, spruce, or fir, you will need to repeat this step at least 3 times, preferably 5 to 7 times. I know it's tedious, but if you want an heirloom, it's imperative.

Step 7. Apply the crackling medium on the areas to be painted. This can be found in most craft stores in the paint section. It is essentially a waxy finish. Then paint on a topcoat of the desired color (5-37). As the paint dries, it will "crack," exposing the darker paint underneath.

5-37 Detail painting is being done by Melissa Honeycutt.

Step 8. Mist a clear finish over the entire figure. If you spray it on too thickly or try to brush on the first coat, your paint will run. For this final clear coat, I like to use a high shine glaze, also found in most craft stores in the paint section. After the first coat has tacked up, you can spray or brush on succeeding coats. It usually takes 2 to 3 coats to get a high shine (refer to 5-I). You may prefer to use a semi-gloss or matte finish. Use whatever you prefer, but you do need to seal your painted surfaces. For figures that will be used on carousels, I spray on 5 to 7 coats of automotive acrylic-enamel clear coat.

Finishing for a Fully-Painted Figure

This section on painting the entire carousel figure is illustrated and written by my daughter, and experienced carousel horse painter, Charity White Saddler, for the original Applebee carved carousel horse that needed to be redone.

Step I. Begin as you would with a figure to be given a natural finish. Sand the entire figure, first with medium-grit sandpaper, then with fine.

Step 2. Seal the figure at this point. I'm painting this figure with a textured surface (5-38).

5-38 Prime the horse with textured paint; the color does not matter.

Once the figure is completely painted and clear coated, this early application of texture adds a lot of depth. The color you use is not important. You are using it for texture, not for color. You will be painting over it. If you are not going to use a textured paint finish, you need to sand and seal, sand and seal, sand and seal, until all scratches and other blemishes are eliminated.

Step 3. Spray or paint on a thin coat of white primer paint (5-39). We call this the "discovery" coat. If you did not use textured paint, you will discover that you missed a lot of scratches, nicks and other blemishes. The white paint will really spotlight all such flaws. Fill in or sand out all the "discovered" flaws using wallboard putty. Primer paint again. I prefer to use a color like gray or tan instead of white for this coat, unless you plan to paint the figure white, because these base coats create an illusion of added depth, and they are easier to cover.

Step 4. Choose at least two colors for the body of the figure: a primary color and a darker color for shadows. You may also choose a lighter color for highlights. Paint the darker color in all muscles,

✒ Painting the Body Colors

Using a damp rag or a very soft brush, blend the light paint outward, into the dark areas. When using a brush, quick "lightly touching" strokes are best. Keep very little paint on the brush for blending the body colors. Dab the excess paint off the brush.

Do the blending when the darker color is almost, but not quite, dry. It is helpful to brush against the direction of the carving and undercuts. A patting motion with the rag also helps you to blend the colors. It is easier to blend the colors on a textured surface than a smooth. If painting with three colors, use a lighter and warmer color for the areas you would touch first when looking straight on, i.e., protruding areas.

undercuts, and any other place you want the horse to be darker or to create shadows (5-40). Paint the lighter color in areas that protrude or where light hits (5-41).

5-39 Primer paint the entire horse with a flat, medium color.

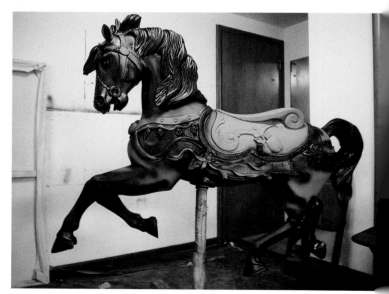

5-40 Paint dark colors into areas where shadows are desired, undercuts, and muscles.

5-41 Blend main/primary, lighter color into darker color on body and mane.

Step 5. Follow the same steps for painting the mane and tail.

Step 6. Select a color scheme for the decorations. You do not have to know precisely every color for every spot before you start; just a couple of colors before you begin. As you progress, more ideas will often come. Be flexible and not afraid to change your mind.

Step 7. Paint all the decorations that you want to be the same color before moving on (5-42). For the first coat, don't worry about shading; it will

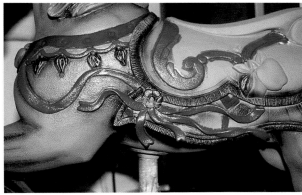

5-42 Paint the decorations. Do all of one color where you desire it. Don't worry about staying in the lines, except up against the completed body. If you get out of the lines, don't worry! It can be fixed.

✒ *Allow Yourself to Experiment*

If mixing your own colors, mix more than you think you will need. Should you miscalculate and need to mix some more, you will never be able to match that shade again. The most important thing is to feel free to experiment and not be afraid to change your mind (5-43, 5-44). Even famous painters go outside the lines and change their minds. It takes practice. Let go and enjoy yourself. Think of the thrill you're going to give a child somewhere. Looking through pictures of other carousel figures can help give you ideas and provide guidelines for where darker areas often are.

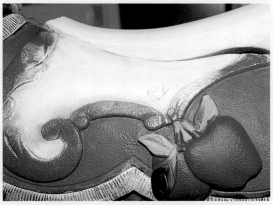

5-43 I decided the red apples did not look good against the burgundy/purple blanket and changed my mind on their color.

5-44 I arrived at gold after trying red and green/red apples. Never hesitate to change your mind and try several different colors if you are unsure.

Painting Techniques for the Decorations

Put a lot of paint on the brush. Use a soft brush, with long bristles, in the largest size you can (5-45). For beginners, choose a brush one size larger than you are naturally inclined to use. The larger the brush, the more paint it can hold and the more area you can cover. Dip the brush in the paint and do not wipe it off. You want to paint your carousel figure, not the side of the can. Simply hold the brush over the container and roll it over until the paint stops dripping.

When applying the paint, take long strokes in one direction. Do not use short feathery strokes, patting, or

5-45 Brushes I like: House brush for primer, body, and mane, including shading. I use the wide flat brush for nearly everything else. I only use the small round brushes on final inspection.

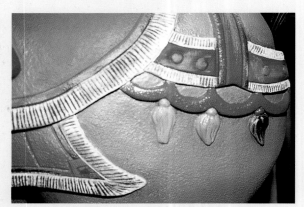

5-46 In areas where you want to show the darker colors underneath, dry brush the lighter color on. Use a soft brush and quick strokes with very little paint on the brush.

tapping once the stroke has reached a point where the paint is not creating a solid line. Dip the brush in the paint again.

You can fairly easily tell an amateur painter from a pro: an amateur will drain most of the paint from the brush against the side of the can, and then use short, feathery back and forth strokes. Time is money and a professional can't waste time with inefficient technique. Short, feathery strokes are only appropriate when you want darker colors underneath to show through (5-46). The professional techniques I have described take a little practice, but once mastered, they save a tremendous amount of time.

If you make a mistake and get more paint in an area than intended, use the damp rag to wipe some away, or let the area dry and start back with the darker color.

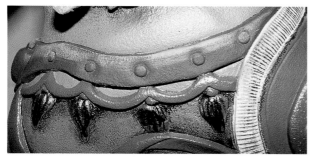

5-47 You can use your finger as a small brush to sweep on highlights in the areas where the light hits first, such as the blue strap.

require a second coat. I like to start painting the area that is most difficult for me. Don't worry about staying in the lines except for where you are painting next to areas that are already completed. Complete all the decorations with one coat before applying any needed second coats. Don't forget the eyes, teeth, tongue and horseshoes.

Step 8. Apply a second coat. Cover all see-through paint. While the paint is still wet, paint a darker cool shade of the same color into the undercut areas and lighter highlights (5-47). Use a dry or mostly dry brush or finger to blend into the primary color. No hard lines.

Choose a lighter, warm color to blend into the raised areas. The areas you would touch first. Don't worry about shading very small areas. If you do, it will just look cluttered.

Step 9. Go back with a small brush and touch up areas where you painted outside the lines. You

5-48 The painted original carving of the Applebee carousel horse, found in over 1,000 Applebee Restaurants worldwide, with its carver, Bruce A. White, and painter, Charity White Saddler.

may need to do this several times. Don't be discouraged; it's normal.

Step 10. Finish with a clear coat spray as described in the "Natural Finish" section (5-48).

◄ Bibliography ◄

Anderson, Sherrel S. *Carousel Horses, a Photographic Celebration.* New York: Running Press, 2000.

Bopp, Ron. *The American Carousel Organ, an Illustrated Encyclopedia.* Matthew Caulfield, Ed. St. Cloud, Minnesota: Palmer Printing, 1998.

Dinger, Charlotte. *Art of the Carousel.* Green Village, New Jersey: Carousel Art, Inc., 1984.

Ellis, Bud and Rhonda Hoeckley. *Carousel Animal Carving, Patterns & Techniques.* New York: Sterling Publishing Co., Inc., 1998.

Fraley, Tobin and Nina Fraley. *The Great American Carousel, a Century of Master Craftsmanship.* New York: Chronicle Books, 1994.

Fried, Frederick. *A Pictorial History of the Carousel.* Vestal, New York: Vestal Press, Ltd., 1964.

Hinds, Anne Dion. *Grab the Brass Ring, the American Carousel.* New York: Crown Publishers, 1990.

Manns, William, Paeggy Shank, Marianne Stevens, Dru Riley, Ed. *Painted Ponies.* Millwood, New York: Zon International Publishing Co., 1987.

Papa, Carrie. *The Carousel Keepers, an Oral History of American Carousels.* New York: McDonald & Woodward Publishing Co., 1998.

Reinhardt, Jerry. *Carving Miniature Carousel Animals, Country Fair Style.* Vestal, New York: Vestal Press. Ltd., 1996.

◄ Metric Equivalents

inches	mm	cm	inches	mm	cm	inches	mm	cm
⅛	3	0.3	4	102	10.2	18	457	45.7
¼	6	0.6	4½	114	11.4	19	483	48.3
⅜	10	1.0	5	127	12.7	20	508	50.8
½	13	1.3	6	152	15.2	21	533	53.3
⅝	16	1.6	7	178	17.8	22	559	55.9
¾	19	1.9	8	203	20.3	23	584	58.4
⅞	22	2.2	9	229	22.9	24	610	61.0
1	25	2.5	10	254	25.4	25	635	63.5
1¼	32	3.2	11	279	27.9	26	660	66.0
1½	38	3.8	12	305	30.5			
1¾	44	4.4	13	330	33.0	inches	feet	m
2	51	5.1	14	356	35.6	12	1	0.305
2½	64	6.4	15	381	38.1	24	2	0.610
3	76	7.6	16	406	40.6	36	3	0.914
3½	89	8.9	17	432	43.2	48	4	1.219

◄ Conversion Factors

mm	=	millimeter						
cm	=	centimeter	1 mm	=	0.039 inch	1 inch	=	25.4 mm
m	=	meter	1 m	=	3.28 feet	1 foot	=	304.8 mm
m^2	=	square meter	$1 m^2$	=	10.8 square feet	1 sq ft	=	0.09 m^2

Cindy 83

Sam the Eagle 70-1

Stark 75　　*Tiger 31*

BRUCE A. WHITE is an internationally known master carver working out of St. Joseph, Missouri. Bruce's wife Cindy assists Bruce in creating his work and running their business, B.W. Carousels and Wildlife. Together they have five children, who also help out.

Bruce has created pieces for Wonder Toys and for the Applebee's restaurant chain, where his carousel horses are featured in over 1,000 restaurants worldwide. He has been commissioned to hand-carve 32 historically accurate replicas to honor master carousel makers from the Golden Age of the Carousel (circa 1879–1929) for the Carnival Heritage Carousel in Kinsley, Kansas funded by the National Foundation for Carnival Heritage. As part of the Carnival Heritage Foundation's annual "Design a Carousel Animal" contest for Kansas students, Bruce continues to finish renditions of the winning entries as part of an entire carousel designed by children. Bruce created his own carousel, the "Wild Thing," which he has donated to the Patee House/Pony Express/Jesse James Museum in his hometown of St. Joseph, Missouri, where it continues to delight children of all ages.

He continues to create original carousel figures on commission, including orders from Chance Rides, Inc., the largest carousel amusement company and the successor to the Allan Herschell companies, based in Whichita, Kansas. His line of endangered species was created for Chance as well as the line of animals sacred to the Aloni Indians that were featured on a carousel for the city of San Jose, California. Reproductions of his carvings are also found on many other carousels, including carousels made by Carousel USA of San Antonio, Texas, Bertalzon Carousels of Milan, Italy, and Luna Park Carousels of Buenes Aires, Argentina. Original carvings by Bruce are found in private collections in the United States, Japan, England and Kuwait. B.W. Carousels and Wildlife can be contacted by e-mail at bwc@stjoelive.com.